INVASION OF THE B-GIRLS

JEWEL SHEPARD

ECLIPSE  BOOKS

Here Are the B-Girls!

On the Cover:
Becky LeBeau is the one in the bikini,
Lisa London is next to her as the country girl,
Kelli Maroney is the cheerleader with the rifle,
Brinke Stevens is the seductive vampire,
Linnea Quigley is the nurse with the meat cleaver,
Monique Gabrielle is the woman in the pink lingerie,
and Jewel Shepard is in the center.

Front and back cover photography by Ken Marcus
Cover design: Visual Strategies, San Francisco

Wardrobe courtesy of Trashy Lingerie, Los Angeles
Make-up by Elizabeth and Shawn
Jewel's hair color by John Patrick of Beverly Hills
Jewel's hair styling by Jim Wayne of Vidal Sassoon, Beverly Hills

Special thanks to:
Mark Evanier, Brent Friedman, Dave Stevens, Jim Wynorski, Mark Borde, Ken Raiche,
Paul Hertzberg and everyone at Cinetel, David DeValle, Jeffrey Assenault, Eric Caidin,
Hollywood Book and Poster Co., Scott Hatch, Jeannine Bisignano-Madsen

INVASION OF THE B-GIRLS © 1992 Jewel Shepard

Eclipse Books
P. O. Box 1099
Forestville, California 95436

First printing March 1992
ISBN 1-56060-158-2

Introduction

One of his letters was ten pages and included a photo and his version of a "Playmate Data Sheet" about himself. Unfortunately, he looked a lot better on the Data Sheet than he did in the photo. He wrote that he liked the way my body looked in "Christina" and told of how he dreamed of us being together, having a picnic in a field. He even included a drawing of the field...rolling hills, trees and, in the center of the picture, a huge cross.

It scared the hell out of me. I had gotten weird letters from fans before but this guy was clearly obsessing on an image he had seen on film...an image that had absolutely nothing to do with me. On and on, he went — relentlessly — about our future life together.

I didn't answer that letter or any of his others. The later ones grew increasingly angry that I had not answered the first. Eventually, he gave up writing, probably turning his affections towards someone else in some other movie. But every time I hear of some actress being hunted down in their home by an obsessive stranger, I wonder about the guy. What makes a man write and propose marriage to an absolute stranger?

Some of the women you'll meet in this book are long-time friends of mine...from movies, acting classes, casting sessions, etc.. Others are new friends...actresses I sought out in an attempt to explore the life and legend of the B-movie starlet. I continue to be amazed at how much we all have in common. Like, almost every one of us has received the above letters.

And almost all of us came from backgrounds heavily-influenced in religion. The lady you see on Cinemax late at night, shedding her clothes in the role of a nymphomaniac nurse...that woman is probably only a few years out of a Catholic all-girls school and Sunday Bible teachings.

And almost all of us live with the same frustrations of Hollywood and the casting system, the same fears of not getting on to better films, more important roles. There is the ever-present worry about growing older. There is a limit to how long you can wear the bikini, do the nude scenes before some casting director says, "She's too old...let's find a new body." There are *always* new bodies.

And almost all of us have a friend or a relative who innocently and incessantly asks — as if we weren't trying — "When are you going to stop making *that kind of movie?*"

There was a time when B-movies were pretty much the same as A-movies but with lower budgets and less well-known stars. The B-movie, as it was originally defined, came about because the double-feature caught on in this country and it wasn't cost effective to make two first-class films to fill out a bill. Many studios converted their old "short subject" divisions over to making cheap features; others picked up and distributed the products of under-financed independent studios. The producers, directors, writers and stars of B-movies were usually either on their way up to making A-films or on their way down from them.

Lacking big budgets, B-movies turned to more "exploitive" themes to add interest. It costs money to build huge sets or fill the stage with dancers. It costs very little to rip a woman's shirt off or show her (seemingly) stabbed with a stiletto. And there is possibly more audience interest in the latter.

In the fifties, studios increasingly began to fill their double-features out by pairing an old A-picture with a new one, leaving no room for the product of all those independents. By the sixties, the major studios were wrestling constantly with the question of how to compete with television...but the B-movie makers already had the answer: Put stuff in movies that they *can't do* on television. And so, "B-movie" came to denote a low budget film that deals, most often, with sexual fantasies and/or violence. Since most of the films are made (or bought) by men, the fantasies tend to be of women removing their clothes and/or being terrorized by chainsaws.

A lot of women who come to Hollywood promise themselves and their families they won't do "that kind" of film. A few manage to have careers and to keep that promise but, for the majority, the day comes when they find that the only available jobs involve nudity or slasher scenes...when they can finally get their elusive Screen Actors Guild card by taking off their top and saying one line...when a lead in a real movie is being dangled and the alternative is a waitressing job. At that point, a woman who wants to act may well make the decision. Someone once asked famed criminal Willie Sutton why he robbed banks. He answered, "Because that's where the money is." When someone asks me why I do B-movies, I answer, "Because that's where the jobs are."

There are a lot of rationales — some of them probably legitimate — for doing the films, many of them offered up by male directors and producers...

"Almost every major actress — from Kim Basinger to Jane Fonda — has done nude scenes..."

"It's a way to get exposure...get your name out there...show people you can handle dialogue..."

"You never know where the people who are making this film will end up. They might wind up making big movies..."

"Low budget movies are a great place to learn your craft..."

"Oh, maybe just this one time...as a favor..."

"I'll put you in my next film and you won't have to take off your clothes..."

And then there's my personal favorite:

"It's just two seconds on the screen."

Right. Two seconds on the screen. Do they know how many people have a V.C.R. with a freeze-frame button? And how many men's magazines will take a frame from the film and publish it as a "celebrity nude?" And what about the still photographer they sneak onto the set to grab publicity shots they can send out?

Still, if you're an actress, you want to act, even if it means playing bimbos and hookers. And some women come to enjoy the attention, the "stardom," the glamour and approval of being someone's sex symbol. At least when they aren't getting letters from weirdos who think they're exactly like the last role they played on screen.

Doing B-movies can be a rough life: Low pay, long hours of shooting, cheap catering, bringing your own wardrobe, sharing a dressing room with others, doing your own make-up or stunts on occasion...all this could be tolerable if it

4

always led to something better but, alas, it does not. Some women find themselves "typed" as B-movie players and are therefore not taken seriously for better roles. Almost everyone I interviewed for this book expressed the frustration of having certain career doors slammed in their faces...and usually not because of their skills or performances but, rather, the very names of the films in which they'd appeared. You can do the best-possible acting job in a low-budget movie but, if they release it under the title, "Revenge of the Ninja Stewardesses," a large segment of Hollywood will simply discount you as an actress. You often find yourself having to joke about the film — put it down, even — to tell the world, "Hey, I don't want to do these films...but this is all that's available to me now."

A number of top actors and actresses have, of course, gotten up and out of B-films, the best example perhaps being Jack Nicholson, who started in Roger Corman's low-budget horror/biker films. Jamie Lee Curtis segued from "Halloween" and a rep as a "scream queen" to A-films. Phoebe Cates has come a long way from "Private School" — as far as Kelly Preston (from "Metalstorm") or Cristina Raines (from "Stacey"). Few of today's big stars do not have a B-role or two in their pasts.

Still, the stigma of the B-movie exists, helped in part by the few actors and actresses who graduated from B-films to A and fiercely deny their pasts. Several actresses — including one of the stars of "Ghoulies II" — declined to be interviewed for this book, insisting they had never done anything but A-films.

I put this book together because I thought it was important for those of us who have done B-films to be able to speak in our own words, not mouthing dialogue written for some chainsaw-wielding cheerleader. Every actress you're about to meet is different: Some are proud of their films and their careers, others pray to live them down. But, as you'll see, we all have certain things in common, as well. I enjoyed talking to all these wonderful ladies and I learned a lot. I hope you enjoy eavesdropping on us.

"I seduce a man at a bar and take him to my room...then I come out with a shower cap and a chainsaw and chew him up into bits."

Michelle Bauer

For a period of several months, years ago, you couldn't go to a newsstand without seeing Michelle Bauer/McClellan staring at you from the men's magazine section. Her tanned physique adorned many a cover and centerfold, prompting a storm of fan mail to the magazines. Those fans were probably delighted, in the years following, to see her turn up in a bevy of B-movies, ranging from the cult X-rated classic, "Cafe Flesh" to a series of cut-rate quickies, as notable for their titles ("Sorority Babes in the Slimeball Bowl-a-Rama") as their content.

JEWEL: Let's start from the beginning...

MICHELLE: I was born in Montebello and raised in Simi Valley, did all my schooling there. Then I got married to Mr. Bauer...

JEWEL: But aren't you married to someone else now?

MICHELLE: I'm on my second marriage. I'm now Michelle McClellan and actually trying to change my name on a few old credits...for instance, on "Hollywood Chainsaw Hookers," I got credit as Michelle McClellan but all the write-ups on it used Michelle Bauer. So I'm slowly trying to make the transition but it's hard. I'm more recognized as Michelle Bauer.

JEWEL: Tell me about your parents.

MICHELLE: My mother is a nursery school teacher in Florida and my father works for a condominium management company in San Diego.

JEWEL: Were they divorced when you were growing up?

MICHELLE: They got divorced when I was quite young. I lived with my mother. I think it had a pretty big effect on my life. Maybe that's where I got the drive for acting, wanting some attention. Maybe that's where my little exhibitionism comes from. *(laughs)*

JEWEL: While we're on that subject...*(laughs)* How did you get into nude magazines?

MICHELLE: Just a fluke. I was looking for a part-time summer job but my ex-husband said I could only do part-time if I made full-time money. I'm thinking, "How am I going to do that?" Well, I saw an ad that said "Figure models wanted for $75 a day." I thought, "Wow!" So I checked into it and found out it was nude figure modeling. I thought about it and thought about it...see I never really felt that confident about myself physically but I figured, "If they want me, give it a try." And I did and it was pretty successful.

JEWEL: You graced quite a lot of covers...*(both Jewel and Michelle share a*

7

laugh) Now did your parents see any of these?

MICHELLE: No, the only magazine they saw and were aware of, from that time on, was a *Penthouse* centerfold I'd done way back when. My mother actually thought it was nice. She thought it was pretty. My father thought it was fine, too, but my siblings didn't think much of it. A few friends even saw it and were kind of excited about it but a lot of people can't see the transition going from magazines into movies. They just see that moment. And actually, I couldn't either at the time. I didn't know what it was going to do for my future.

JEWEL: What were you telling people your occupation was?

MICHELLE: Whatever popped into my head! *(laughs)* Oh, I'm a part-time secretary or whatever...but I never told anyone about it. I felt that was real personal. I guess I felt a little ashamed doing it. Eventually, I even developed a bad attitude about the whole thing and that's when I left the print agency I was with.

JEWEL: Did you ever see yourself in liquor stores?

MICHELLE: Oh, Jewel, it really bothered me after a while. I felt like I violated myself, like I put myself there. And I started asking myself "Why did I do that?"

JEWEL: What did your first husband think about it?

MICHELLE: You know, he didn't even care. He'd hold out his hand and say, "How much money'd you make today?" But my husband now...when we first started living together, he said, "Please, don't do *Penthouse*. Don't do those things anymore. Just get on with the movie thing. Get an agent!" So I did.

JEWEL: Why did you get a boob job?

MICHELLE: I didn't like what I was born with. It was a very difficult decision to make because it was shortly after my transition into movies and I was getting more magazine offers, but that wasn't the point. It was for me. My big question was, and I didn't know then because I was so far away from having a child, but I wanted to breast-feed. I was just very interested in how it was going to affect my life.

JEWEL: Do you get recognized a lot?

MICHELLE: No, I really don't get recognized because I've made a point not to be dressed-up or made-up when I went out. I was always very incognito in public. Never curled my hair or anything...but you know what just happened to me recently? It was just after I had my baby...I went out with my girlfriend and left my husband at home with the baby. I got all dolled up: curled my hair, put on make up and a sexy dress...Well, this man asked me to dance. So I said fine. Now, I had been out of circulation, out of the movies, for over a year and half. Magazines were years ago! But this guy recognized me from some magazine phone sex ads. My jaw just dropped.

JEWEL: How did you feel?

MICHELLE: Terrible. I went home and cried.

JEWEL: But you never did any pornos, did you? Nothing to really feel terrible about?

MICHELLE: I did "Cafe Flesh" because I loved the script, but I insisted that they use doubles for the sex scenes. And it was very obvious. I even got fan mail asking if I was doubled.

JEWEL: "Cafe Flesh" is a cult classic! What did you do in that?

MICHELLE: I was one of the leads. The story is about the sex positives and

the sex negatives after the nuclear bomb has dropped, the people who could have sex and those who couldn't. I was one of the ones that could, but I didn't tell anybody until Johnny Rico came to town...and I couldn't hold back any longer *(laughs)*. But I never put that one on my résumé because it did get an "X" rating.

JEWEL: Let's hear some of the other films you've been in.

MICHELLE: Well, most currently..."Beverly Hills Vampire," which was a Fred Olen Ray film. Britt Ekland was the lead vampire and I was one of her three vampirettes. It was a lot of fun. Fred Olen is a wonderful person. He makes movie-making fun. Same with Dave Dakota.

JEWEL: What's another one?

MICHELLE: Well, "Sorority Babes in the Slimeball Bowl-A-Rama." Brinke Stevens and I were a couple of sorority babes who are getting initiated by having to go with these nerds to a bowling alley and break in. But we run into Linnea Quigley, who's the bad girl. She's this punk who's breaking into the cash register and we run into her and break this trophy that has an imp in it who grants wishes that go bad. So we all die, everybody except Linnea and the other lead.

JEWEL: One more...

MICHELLE: Then there was "Hollywood Chainsaw Hookers," which I also did with Linnea. The chainsaw comes in when I seduce a man at a bar and take him to my room, get him going by dancing around, get him all excited. Then I make him close his eyes and come out with a shower cap and a chainsaw and chew him up into bits. But it wasn't very gory, just funny. See, we're a cult. We're these hookers that go out and get victims so we can sacrifice them to the god Annubis, who we worship. Linnea does the dance of the chainsaw and kills our master, which breaks me out of my trance and we have this big battle where she kills me *(laughs)*. My mother loves these movies. She gets a big kick out of them.

JEWEL: Don't you ever get a chill when you see yourself get killed on screen?

MICHELLE: Not if it's a comedy-horror film. That's different compared to something like "Demon Warp" where I got my heart ripped out. That was almost gruesome. And "Lady Avenger," I got shot with a gun, but then that was justifiable because the character deserved to be shot.

JEWEL: Are you selective about how you choose your films? Or will you do anything?

MICHELLE: I'm pretty picky as to what I would do...there was this one film, "Rollerblade 2," which had this graphic rape scene that I didn't want to do. See, I had done "Rollerblade" but that was a bit part and I told the producers that there was a better way to do the scene and make it less graphic. But they thought that scene was a major selling point for the film.

JEWEL: Describe the rape scene.

MICHELLE: It was a mutant girl who couldn't speak. She was a good force, sort of angelic, who gets captured and raped by these thugs. The producers kept telling me it would be real fun but I turned it down. It just went against my own personal standards of what a film should be...

JEWEL: Do your fans ever scare you?

MICHELLE: There's this one guy in Canada who writes this stuff like, "Your body is a love temple!" I just write him back on a very normal level. I don't feed the fire, I just write "Thank you very much" and send him nice, smiley pictures of myself.

JEWEL: By any chance, have you ever done any boob war* stuff?

MICHELLE: Yeah, I did a couple of those. They were these things for private collectors where I just turned my mind off and went to work. They weren't real outlandish, maybe just a little strange. They just wanted us to do these funny things.

JEWEL: Do you feel like those kind of things, and maybe even the magazine stuff you did, could ever come back to haunt you?

MICHELLE: No. If anything it helped, as much as I hate to say it. A lot of people say, "Any publicity is good publicity...even bad publicity." It gets me recognized.

JEWEL: So are you officially retired?

MICHELLE: No. I would love to continue working. In fact, I just contacted Dave Dakota and Fred Olen Rey and told them I wanted to continue. It was a big question mark for me having a family, but I'm finding I want to get back into it. Also, a lot of films I had just done before the baby are now coming out, like "Assault of the Party Nerds."

JEWEL: *(laughs)* I can't wait to hear what you did in that one...

MICHELLE: Linnea and I played these weird little bimbos who go out with these jocks that turned out to be gay lovers. So we go out with the nerds and find out it's not so great to be jockettes.

JEWEL: Was that another Fred Olen Rey picture?

MICHELLE: "Assault of the Party Nerds" was actually done by Richard Gabai, who I met on "Nightmare Sisters."

JEWEL: *(laughs)* "Nightmare Sisters"?

MICHELLE: That was with Brinke, Linnea and me as these nerdy girls who couldn't get dates. Brinke had her hair pulled back and horn-rimmed glasses,

---

* *The "Boob War" tapes are videos made for private collectors, usually revolving around a simple plot: Topless women arguing over whose breasts are larger. For more on this, see Becky LeBeau's interview.*

Linnea had these buck teeth and freckles and Ken Hall made me a fat suit. I was 250 pounds! *(laughs)* There was this one scene, an outtake actually, where we get these nerds to come over and Linnea opens the door to greet them and her buck teeth go flying across the room. It was hysterical!

JEWEL: How much do you make on these pictures?

MICHELLE: Most of them are real low budget...something like $75 a day. You don't get much, but that isn't the point...speaking for myself. When Fred calls me and says "I've got this great part, let's do it," I do it.

JEWEL: Don't you ever sit back and worry about what's best for your career?

MICHELLE: I don't think of it that way. I think of it as "here and now." I just want to have fun. I know there'll be a day when I can't do this any more, but for now I just want to get while the gettin's good. *(laughs)* I mean, right now I have a husband with his own business and a daughter and that gives me a great deal of self-satisfaction.

JEWEL: Do you ever read for mainstream movies? And do the casting people ever raise an eyebrow over some of the stuff you've done?

MICHELLE: Not really. They're amused by the titles, I guess, but they're just looking for experience...I mean, most of the films I've done are just so much fun. It's like family when you work with Fred and Dave.

JEWEL: Who do you really look up to?

MICHELLE: I'd have to say Raquel Welch, because she was one of the first sex symbols that showed she could do more than be beautiful.

JEWEL: Do you worry about what your daughter will think of your career?

MICHELLE: I worry about that but when the time comes, I'll just sit down and tell her. I'll be as open as I can. I just want her to have her own judgments about it. Hopefully, she can look at me when I'm old and wrinkled and maybe be enlightened by the whole thing.

"I was a 'Bond Girl.' Anyone associated with the Bond movies was a 'Bond Girl.'"

Martine Beswicke

With the supreme success of the James Bond films in the sixties came a new classification for the film world's glamour girls. To the tradition of the Mack Sennett Bathing Beauties and the Goldwyn Girls was now added "The Bond Girls." Every 007 picture had several, some with dialogue, some killed, some written-in specifically to service the publicity department's lust to plant magazine layouts. It was as a Bond girl that filmgoers first met Martine Beswicke: That got her the fame and rep. Now, all she had to do was prove — as so many of the Bond Girls couldn't — that she could act and do more than drape the villain's poolside area. This, she proved on several continents — with a series of films shot in Italy and Great Britain; then she migrated to America for a steady regimen of film and TV roles. Well past the stage where an actress is hired on looks alone, Martine could well serve as the perfect example of an actress triumphing over the frequent query of "Yeah, she's beautiful...but can she act?"

JEWEL: Based on your accent, I'm assuming you didn't grow up in this country.

MARTINE: I was born in Port Antony, Jamaica. My mother was basically a housewife. And I have this very romantic picture of my father. He sort of roamed the estate of my grandfather, overseeing the plantation. My grandfather owned a lot of land and estates. It was great, growing up there. I have a lot of fond memories.

JEWEL: Was the school system the same as it is here?

MARTINE: No. It's more like the British school system. High school goes from eight to sixteen, then you take an equivalence test. But I only went there four years, and it was hard enough to keep me in the classroom for that long. I was always dreaming.

JEWEL: What were you dreaming about?

MARTINE: About far, foreign lands. I read a lot of books. I love to read these wonderful romantic novels.

JEWEL: That's funny because most people think of Jamaica as a far-away, romantic land.

MARTINE: But my grandfather traveled a lot, and he would come back with exotic stories from other countries, expensive wines and beautiful textiles. He loved fine living and he trained me to appreciate these things. He made me a little princess.

JEWEL: So after four years of schooling, what happened?

MARTINE: Well, my mother decided that her two little princesses — and that's the way she thought of us — were going to be taken to the mother country and educated. But I still didn't stay the duration. I wasn't happy, because I wanted to act. See, I wanted to act from the time I was four years old.

JEWEL: Now where was your father during all this?

MARTINE: Oh, my parents had divorced when I was eight. But I was very grown-up about it. I remember being teased by the other kids about my parents being divorced, to which I stood up and said: "If two people do not get on, I see no reason why they should have to stay together."

JEWEL: You said you wanted to act way back at age four. How did you know? What inspired you?

MARTINE: Actually, I remember when I was two and they started taking pictures of me, I cried every time. They have pictures of me literally running away from the camera. Then, at age four or so, I came around and became an absolute ham in front of the camera. And even though I'd never seen a film, I knew I wanted to be an actress. I don't know how I knew. I just did.

JEWEL: Do you remember what film you saw first?

MARTINE: Charlie Chaplin films. We used to have movies set up in our backyard for all the kids to come and watch.

JEWEL: What did your parents think of acting as a profession?

MARTINE: Well, at thirteen, my mother asked me if I was truly serious, and I said, "Yes. I have to be an actress." So she made a compromise. She let me pursue it but insisted that I go to secretarial school in the evening for something to fall back on. And I didn't mind because there were no uniforms or anything, and it was much better than regular school.

JEWEL: When did you get your first acting job?

MARTINE: Well, after a brief stint as a secretary, my mother decided that she had her hands full and took us back to Jamaica. And since I was too young, I couldn't stay. So when I got back, I started modeling. There was a little circle of us...the prettiest girls from the best families. We did a lot of tourist type stuff. Anyway, a producer came down to Jamaica and started looking for a girl to be his star. He thought I was just the cat's knickers. And he put me on film in my bikini, which really spurred me on...then it turns out that he showed the footage to a huge agency in England. They wrote me and said if I was ever over there to give them a call. So, a year later, I took them up on the offer. It was just when they started casting the first Bond, "Dr. No."

JEWEL: Did they actually audition you for the Ursula Andress role?

MARTINE: Yes, but I didn't have any background or experience. The director told me, though, that he was doing the next Bond film and that I could be in that one.

JEWEL: Was that "From Russia with Love"?

MARTINE: Yes. I played a fighting gypsy. It was a small, but pivotal role...I was so nervous, I got laryngitis.

JEWEL: You must've been in awe, working with Sean Connery.

MARTINE: Actually, the Bond explosion hadn't really hit yet and Sean was just starting out, too.

JEWEL: What were the sixties like for you?

MARTINE: I loved it. I am so glad I had that. The eighties were really tough...I had a lot of fun in the sixties. It was the beginning of the discotheque scene and I was a "Bond Girl." Anyone associated with the Bond movies was a "Bond Girl." There was a whole group of us traveling in the same circle. Michael

Martine Beswicke, Sean Connery and Luciana Paluzzi on the set of "Thunderball" (1965)

Caine, Terence Stamp...we were all young.

JEWEL: Now, had you stopped modeling?

MARTINE: No, in-between "Dr. No" and "From Russia..." I worked "prettying up sets" for TV shows. They wanted high class looking extras, you see. So I would show up and get a line or two, but it was basically modeling.

JEWEL: After "From Russia..." you did "Thunderball"?

MARTINE: When "Thunderball" came up, they didn't want to use me because you don't use a Bond Girl twice. They had this bad line about us being "dispensable." Finally, Terence [Hill, the director] convinced Cubby Broccoli and Harry Saltzman that I should play the Island Girl. "Thunderball" is one of my favorite film memories. Bond had just hit, massively. I remember it was July in Nassau and the place was swarming with kids who wanted to see the filming...plus, a lot of the people associated with the film brought their yachts down. And there was this one scene where they tried to use all the millionaires of the world as extras! And everywhere the cast went, everyone wanted to have us for dinner. The governor, the this, the that...we were in high demand. It was great!

JEWEL: Were you overwhelmed by all this?

MARTINE: You have to remember, I grew up in money. And my mother always said I was a princess. So there I was, totally deserving of it.

JEWEL: How did you get "One Million Years B.C.?"

MARTINE: After the Bond films, they were coming to me...it was a bigger part for me. I was the Pig Woman.

JEWEL: Did it bother you that in all your films thus far you were rarely wearing more than a couple pieces of cloth?

MARTINE: I kind of liked my body at the time, and I also liked the power of it. So I thought, "What the hell?" I just pushed ahead.

JEWEL: You did "Prehistoric Women" next. Weren't you afraid of being typecast as a Neanderthal?

MARTINE: In those days, one of the most important things in our lives was to have fun. And that movie just sounded like a lot of fun. I remember that on the set of "One Million..." the producer said he had another movie for me. He said, "I want you to be my queen!" I said, "I am. How perfect!" I loved the idea...I was the evil queen who gave away these little blonde girls as part of a sacrifice for a white rhinoceros. Only the blondies went, though. The darkies were my hench-women. *(laughs)*

JEWEL: Did your family see any of these films when they first came out?

MARTINE: Well, they were mostly back in Jamaica so they didn't see them for years later. But they were awfully proud.

JEWEL: Tell me about "The Penthouse."

MARTINE: That one was really tough. I'd been doing a lot of work. I was getting stretched out. This friend of mine who had done a lot of TV got together his first feature and asked me to play this part called Harry, who had pages and pages of monologues. I said, "I can't do this!" But he said to me, "What have you been doing? Acting! You can act! It's perfect for you!"

JEWEL: What was this film called?

MARTINE: "Tom, Dick and

"Il Bacio" (1973)

Harry." It's about a guy who puts his mistress up in an isolated penthouse and two metermen come to the door and tie up the man and rape the mistress. And the metermen keep talking about how Harry is waiting down in the car. This couple is terrified, thinking that there's a third man down there. So I come up and pretend that I'm a probation officer and that the couple has escaped. The whole thing gets rather nasty.

JEWEL: What was the story behind "Dr. Jekyll and Sister Hyde?"

MARTINE: Well, I'd come to America in the midst of all these films. I'd fallen in love with John Richardson on "One Million...", and he lived in America. So I came with him and stayed here, starting to do TV and concentrating on raising my acting to another level by working with Lee Strasberg and Peggy Feury, Stella Adler and such. I worked a lot, doing mostly TV. But when I took a vacation back to England, I went in to see my old friends at Hammer. They said they'd been waiting for me, looking for me to play this part, "Dr. Jekyll and Sister Hyde." I said, "I love it!" It was just the story of the male and female clashing. Unfortunately, Hammer was becoming very exploitational at the time. They wanted a lot of nudity, even full frontal nudity — which wasn't even in the script! That created a real rift between the director and myself, but it all worked out. I'm just sorry they didn't take the idea more seriously.

JEWEL: How do you feel about doing nudity?

MARTINE: I never had a problem with it, but I did have a problem with how they treated it. I remember on "Jekyll..." it was supposed to be a closed set and there was standing room only. People were hanging from the rafters. But I just didn't let it bother me. I knew they could look, but they couldn't touch.

JEWEL: You did Oliver Stone's first film, "Seizure." How was it working with Oliver, compared say, to some of the British directors you've worked with?

MARTINE: By the time I did "Seizure," I was living in Rome. John Richardson and I had separated. Since there was no work in England, I went where the work was. Now, I hadn't been over there more than a couple months when I got a call from the states saying that Oliver Stone has seen me in "Jekyll..." and wanted me for his movie. So I came back and got the part, sight unseen. I joined them in Canada. He was kind of insane. He would sacrifice anything for a shot. But I loved his sort of maniacal side. The movie, in fact, was based on one of his nightmares and it was like the cast and crew were living out this nightmare!

JEWEL: You worked with another infamous director, Fred Olen Ray, on

"Cyclone." How was that?

MARTINE: You couldn't really take it too seriously. We'd get on the set and he'd say, "Well, who wants to say something?" He just kind of threw a script together, but it was more of a guideline.

JEWEL: You went from such big movies, the "Bond" movies, to the lower budget pictures you seem to be doing now. Why is that?

MARTINE: One can't be too choosy at this point. I'm caught in between. I'm too old to be young and too young to be old. I don't fit into the image that people have of me, which is the old image of me: Bond Girl, queen, killer. So I have to shift the perspective of who I am. But I take responsibility for the situation I'm in now. Today's young actors know that this is a business and treat it that way. When I started, it was all sort of a game.

JEWEL: Is there anything you would've liked to do differently?

MARTINE: If I had my druthers, I would have started plotting and planning my career from the beginning. But at the time in the sixties, I was just in for having a good time.

JEWEL: How do you feel about yourself now?

MARTINE: I'm a very spiritual person. I've taken some seminars designed to help me look at myself and see how to balance it. It's a lifelong task, but I feel I've gotten much closer to myself in the last few years. I haven't gotten closer to making a whole lot of money as a star but...a friend of mine said something so beautiful about me to another girl, who asked, "Why isn't Martine a bigger star?" And my friend said, "You know, Martine is really amazing at just being human." I think that's the bottom line to who I am right now.

20th Century Fox presents

PREHISTORIC WOMEN

COLOR By DeLUXE

starring
MARTINE BESWICK · EDINA RONAY · MICHAEL LATIMER · MICHAEL CARRERAS · HENRY YOUNGER
A SEVEN ARTS-HAMMER Production · CINEMASCOPE

Produced and Directed by   Screenplay by

"I remember thinking that it was going to get me more interviews, but it didn't. I suppose I became the girl who would do a few lines and take her clothes off."

Monique Gabrielle

She was on screen for less than a minute in the film "Bachelor Party" but she still has to endure identification as the girl in the bedroom scene — this, despite the fact that Monique Gabrielle has become one of the most-employed ladies in Hollywood in the last few years. For a time, she was typed in nude roles — an unfortunate side effect of "Bachelor Party" and a centerspread as a *Penthouse* "pet" — but is now racking up some impressive credits in clothed roles that require considerable acting.

JEWEL: You have a very interesting look. What's your ethnic background?

MONIQUE: Spanish, Scotch-Irish, French, German, Danish, Dutch and English.

JEWEL: Where were you born?

MONIQUE: I was born in Kansas City, Missouri, but then I moved at the age of two to Denver, Colorado.

JEWEL: What did your parents do?

MONIQUE: I don't know what they did back then. My father is disabled now and my mother is a cafeteria manager at Montgomery-Ward's.

JEWEL: So you grew up in Denver?

MONIQUE: Yeah. My grandparents lived in Denver, so that's why we moved out there. My mother wanted to be near them.

JEWEL: Were you a popular girl?

MONIQUE: No. I was always the odd one. I was kind of odd looking and I had an odd sense of humor. I was always really sarcastic, and I used to make fun of myself before others could.

JEWEL: Did other kids tease you a lot?

MONIQUE: Yeah, they called me "Ugly Dog." And I had a volatile temper so I'd fly off the handle. They also called me "Witch," but I'm sure they meant "Bitch." This was a private school — a Christian school that I attended from 7th to 11th grade. But they didn't have the best Christian attitude...they were spoiled rotten rich kids. So if you were a little different and didn't come from money, you were an outcast. And I didn't want to do what everybody did. I didn't want to follow anybody...I wanted to work instead of go to school. I took voice lessons. I wanted to act and sing. I even skipped school a lot so I could stay home and write songs or stories. I wasn't interested in school. But there wasn't much use for developing entertainment talents in Colorado.

JEWEL: What inspired you to become an actress?

MONIQUE: I wish I knew. There is something I remember...when I was four or five I was an angel in a church pageant and I had these little wings. I just liked the audience and how they applauded afterwards. I appreciated the attention.

JEWEL: I see that you have a lot of beauty pageant trophies.

MONIQUE: Yeah, I participated in a number of contests like the "Miss Hollywood" pageant. But some of the them were smaller things like "Miss Travel."

JEWEL: But still, you mentioned that you always felt "odd" growing up, and that your peers called you names like "Ugly Dog." Did winning beauty contests vindicate you to some degree?

MONIQUE: I was always admired by outsiders. Photographers started asking me if I was a model at around the age of fifteen...and the kids at school knew I was modeling because they saw my pictures. But that didn't change their attitudes. In fact, it just gave them something else to tease me about.

JEWEL: What did you do after high school?

MONIQUE: I knew I wanted to act and I knew I was going to end up in California but my parents wanted me to have something to fall back on so I applied to a school in Dallas that specialized in fashion merchandising. But then my parents decided to move to California and it hit me that'd I'd be in Dallas and they'd be where I wanted to be. So I said, "Forget school. I'm going to California. I'm going to be discovered and they're going to make me a big star!" I guess that's what everybody thinks when they first come out here...

JEWEL: So what did you do when you first got out here?

MONIQUE: I made a major mistake. I looked in the classified section of the L.A. Times because they list some modeling and acting jobs, but most of them aren't that legitimate. Anyway, I got in with a modeling school agency in Orange County. And after about two months, they sent me to Japan because a girl ahead of me had dropped out. So I went, and during the day, you modeled and at night, you did go-go dancing. It was the greatest learning experience of my life. I learned to deal with certain kinds of men, like our boss who wanted to sleep with all of us. You learn how to get out of the situation without insulting him. You need to know that stuff when you get to California.

JEWEL: So when you did get back here, what was your next move?

MONIQUE: I studied at an actor's workshop for a while. They also had modeling classes. And on the first night, the modeling teacher said I already knew everything. Eventually, I helped her out, and even took over her class, which got me my classes for free. Anyway, they had a connection with an extra agency. So I did that on a couple movies. I took my picture with the stars, told the director how much I wanted to be an actress; I did all the things you always hear about people doing to get a line, but that didn't happen.

JEWEL: So how did you get your Screen Actors Guild card?

MONIQUE: After I'd been in California about a year and a half, I got a manager. But he was under the impression that you can make a girl into a star by making her into a sex symbol first. So he got me into the whole T-and-A scene. But I didn't know anything and it sounded like a good gameplan to me.

JEWEL: Now, did the idea of nudity bother you?

MONIQUE: Not really. And although my mother is fairly strict, my father has an open attitude about nudity. He's a nudist. So the way I was brought

up, I was never treated like nudity is a big deal. I saw my parents nude all the time. And because I was fairly comfortable being nude around my family, it wasn't too bad being nude in front of other people. Also, after all those years of being repressed and not the center of attention, this was my chance to get people to look at me. I felt great! People were doing my make-up and fussing over me.

JEWEL: Getting back to my earlier question, what was the first film to get you your S.A.G. card?

MONIQUE: It was "Young Doctors in Love." It was directed by a fantastic director, Garry Marshall. And Jerry Bruckheimer produced it. I ended up getting cut out of the movie, but I had a topless scene with one of the actors. I had mixed feelings about being cut out, though, because I hadn't told my parents yet that I was doing nudity.

JEWEL: What was your next film?

MONIQUE: I did "Night Shift." And the nudity I did stayed in the

"Transylvania Twist" (1990)

film and my parents did see it. That was directed by another wonderful man, Ron Howard. Because both those films were big budgets, everyone was very nice and respectful to me.

JEWEL: Then you did "Bachelor Party," right?

MONIQUE: I had originally gone in to read for a larger part, but they rewrote the script and gave me this other part, the part of Tracy. They were paying me a lot of money, so I was excited. There was one funny incident...there was a stand-up comedian who was extremely obnoxious. He tried to hit on every girl and for some reason totally latched onto me. So I have to work and deal with this guy's chauvinistic attitude all day. Anyway, after we'd been working about twelve hours I'm waiting for them to set up and he comes in and backs me against the wall. So I picked up a belt with a big buckle and told him if he came near me, I'd hit him. He backed off at first but then came at me again. So I punched him in the stomach. The director had to break it up because we got into a little tussle. But the next day on the set, all the other girls applauded me because they had obviously been harassed by him as well.

JEWEL: "Bachelor Party" was a real success, and you were getting noticed for your performance. How did that feel?

MONIQUE: It was pretty exciting. I was getting fan mail for the first time. People still remember my part in that movie, they say, "Oh, you were Tracy! I loved you in that movie! You're a great actress!"

JEWEL: But in your heart you must've know that there wasn't a whole lot of acting in that role, it was more just taking off your clothes. Did you consider what your next step would be?

MONIQUE: Not really. I remember thinking that it was going to get me more interviews, but it didn't. I suppose I became the girl who would do a few lines and take her clothes off. The one nice thing that did come from it was, the people from "Magnum, P.I." saw me in the film and asked me to audition. I didn't get the part, but it was nice to know that it wasn't just the average Joe who saw me in that movie, but a lot of the industry people as well.

JEWEL: After "Bachelor Party," what was next?

MONIQUE: I did a couple of video movies...one was called "E. Nick Vanacuzzi: Legend In His Own Mind." It was sort of star-studded. It had some people from TV and stuff...Jonathan Winters, Skip Stephenson. This was actually the first movie made specifically for the home video market. They thought it was going to be a huge success, but it bombed miserably. Stereotyped again, I play a centerfold.

JEWEL: Which is also what you played in "Amazon Women on the Moon." But at least that was a much bigger movie.

MONIQUE: Actually, I didn't really want to do it because there wasn't a lot of money involved. Plus, it was a completely nude role — except for the TV version where I wear lingerie. I just thought, "Gosh, is this what I want to do?" It was fine when I was doing "Bachelor Party," but I started wondering, "When are they going to take me seriously?" I knew I had to change over but I finally decided to do the part because of all the names involved...John Landis, Joe Dante.

JEWEL: So how did you go from working with big names, to doing low budget B-movies?

MONIQUE: Actually, I always had a problem with agents. It wasn't that I suddenly did lesser films, it was that in between these bigger budget projects, I was doing B-movie stuff that only the diehard fans knew about.

JEWEL: But wasn't it harder to do nudity in low budget movies? Didn't you get that sense of "Where am I going with this?"

MONIQUE: Well, I did a movie with Jim Wynorski called "Death-stalker II" and I was the lead. It was the first lead I'd ever had. I had major dialogue, and not only that, I played dual characters. So it was a great acting challenge. But you're right, things were different. I did complain a lot. We were in Argentina, which is not the greatest place to shoot a film...it certainly wasn't a posh set like the bigger budget films I'd done. But I really did think that this film would make a major difference...unfortunately it never made it to the theaters. Nobody knew about it and nobody cared about it. It didn't change my career, but it was a really fun experience.

JEWEL: You also did "Hot Moves." Was that a positive experience?

MONIQUE: Yeah, because I got to play a ditzy character for once. But it only lasted in the theaters for a week. There was nudity in that one too, but there was actually more of me clothed than nude.

JEWEL: Tell me about "Transylvania Twist."

MONIQUE: In that movie, we make fun of almost every horror film ever made...I play a vampire, the daughter of Robert Vaughn, who's the main vampire. Teri Copely goes to Transylvania, where her father died, and she encounters Vaughn and his three demented vampire daughters, of which I was in charge. It was fun, over-the-top comedy. It played here for about a week, but without a lot of advertising.

JEWEL: Have you done any straight-out horror films?

MONIQUE: I did "Return of the Swamp Thing," but that was more action/adventure than horror. I played a mercenary. It was the first time I played a really tough character and my personality really changed when I picked up a big gun. Suddenly it was like, "I've got power and I'm bitchen!" This was another one I thought would do better than it did...but it will probably do well on video and cable, which is where the first one made money.

JEWEL: Doesn't it frustrate you when something you work so hard on fails

"Deathstalker II" (1987)

to generate interest?

MONIQUE: Well, it gets me thinking, because I don't want to be still doing the same things ten years from now because it'll be awfully hard to compete with the young girls with their perfect bodies. And I can't imagine having kids: "So, mommy, are you going to do another nude scene today?"

JEWEL: Have you ever encountered the casting couch scenario?

MONIQUE: I've never had anyone say directly, "If you want this part, this is what you have to do." I have been pursued by producers and directors. I've had a producer talk about an upcoming project, then in his next breath ask to come home with me. But never once have they directly tied the two together...I did have one instance where a director-producer grabbed my hand and held it to his crotch and said: "See how hard you make me!"

JEWEL: What did you do?

MONIQUE: I tried to get out of there as fast as I could. But at the same time it's so hard to walk that fine line where you don't give in to them, and yet still not insult them. Because they might hire you in the future if you don't sleep with them, but certainly not if you insult them as well.

JEWEL: Have you explored other facets of the entertainment industry to supplement acting?

MONIQUE: Right now I'm trying to do some singing, which I've always liked but have never tried since I came to California. I'm working with someone who produces and we're trying to come up with a dance single. Hopefully something will come from that...Also, I'd like to do something like Becky LeBeau is doing. I mean, after years of being exploited, I'd like to be able to exploit myself.

JEWEL: Are there any causes you feel strongly about?

MONIQUE: I haven't really become physically involved in anything, but I donate money to Greenpeace. I would like to find something, a charity maybe, that I could actually get involved with. I am Pro-Choice, and that's because I think it's better to stop a few lives before they start then let those kids grow up only to be abandoned or abused or who knows what? How will they have a chance to succeed?

JEWEL: Do you feel like you've succeeded in accomplishing what you set out to do?

MONIQUE: I feel that I've done pretty well, but I haven't really accomplished what I wanted. I really wanted to be a major star by now to, you know, show them all. But I don't really have the power I wanted...I know that my high school reunion is coming up and I wonder what they know about me? And I wonder what they're all doing. I'm sure that all the really popular girls are no longer as beautiful with two or three kids hanging off of them. And they probably all really envy me now.

"...it's truly a shame that there are such stupid girls in this town!"

Haji

Skin flick *doyen* Russ Meyer is notorious for employing a male stock company in his films but discarding leading ladies like empty film cans. One of the few exceptions to this practice is the mysterious Haji. In addition to the film credits mentioned below, Haji appeared in a brief cameo in Meyer's legendary "Beyond the Valley of the Dolls." Recently, the U.C.L.A. Film Department screened a well-spliced print of the film to a turn-away crowd and Haji appeared, along with Meyer, screenwriter Roger Ebert and much of the cast before a cheering audience to answer questions.

JEWEL: Is Haji your real name?

HAJI: Yes. It came from my uncle, who was an artist.

JEWEL: Where were you born?

HAJI: I'm really only a visitor here. I was never born, I just came here. I'm not really an earthling.

JEWEL: Uh...when did you realize this?

HAJI: Well, my mother was an earthling, but my father sort of wasn't. She had other children, but when my father married her, I just, you know, "appeared." I've just been here with my mother trying to be an earthling, which hasn't been very easy. I'm still trying to find the earthling style...

JEWEL: Hmmm. Are these beliefs based on some sort of religion?

HAJI: It's been based on my upbringing which is very in touch with nature and instincts. It's called "The Fairness of Life." I find that a lot of earthlings have religion to maintain their endurance, but we believe it's just the power of life. As you would worship your God, we communicate with air.

JEWEL: So was it your mother or father who told you about your, uh, heritage?

HAJI: It was my mother, but it was also something I just kind of realized. She would tell me things, like about human conception, but she would also tell me I couldn't tell other little girls because their parents would be telling them something different. You have to understand, in my time, little girls actually believed that a stork brought babies. This caused me to grow up very secretive, but also very observant. I like to experience things, except anything that will take control of me, like drugs.

JEWEL: Did you get to spend a lot of time with your father?

HAJI: Well, he would just appear every so often, then disappear. But my mother was very much in love with him and he with her. So I was a love child.

JEWEL: You certainly didn't have a normal childhood.

HAJI: No, I didn't go to school like most. I used to just go into the woods because I have this affair with nature. They used to make me go to a psychiatrist to see what was wrong with me.

RUSS MEYER Associates *Present*

Faster, PUSSYCAT! KILL! KILL!

SUPERWOMEN!

STARRING
TURA SATANA • HAJI • Lori **WILLIAMS**
Directed by RUSS MEYER • An EVE Production

JEWEL: And what did the doctors determine?

HAJI: They said to just leave me alone. They found something very different about me and said school would only screw me up. I also used to travel a lot when I was in my early teens. My mother would just put me on a train and I would explore. I learned a lot about self-respect...when I was fourteen, I was out earning $147 a week doing burlesque dancing. That's a lot of money for a girl who didn't even have an education. I had a daughter shortly after that, and I took care of my mother.

JEWEL: It must've been difficult raising a daughter at such a young age, especially with no husband.

HAJI: It was. And I regret that I was too strict. You see, I have a special awareness about people. I know when they are telling the truth and when they are not. My daughter was an earthling and I feared for her. From my own experiences, I knew what people wanted to do to us! So I kept her too busy to go out there in the world. My problem is that I love my daughter too much.

JEWEL: What did your daughter do when you told her where you were from?

HAJI: She just knows it...but most people just think it's a Hollywood gag.

JEWEL: So you were a burlesque dancer. How did you like that?

HAJI: I couldn't believe I was getting paid that much money just to dance. We didn't even take that much off back then! Also, my mother used to take me nude swimming all the time and I had an uncle who was a nude painter, so to take off my clothes and get paid for it was great. I was very happy.

JEWEL: But you were so young...Did the customers ever suggest going somewhere with them after the shows?

HAJI: Oh, yes. I didn't know at the time, but I was a pimp. Guys would ask me to go with them but I would decline. Then in the dressing room, I would tell the other girls what I was offered and they would say, "Let me go!" So I would say, "Okay." After a while I started arranging it with the girls, and the guys would give me ten dollars for setting it up.

JEWEL: How did you make the transition from burlesque to acting?

HAJI: Well, I did belly dancing in-between, but I didn't like it when they shoved tips down my clothes. I hate when men think they're in a fruit stand! "Oh, this is an orange, I'll take it! This is a plum, I want it!" They just grab and touch and feel.

JEWEL: When did you get hooked up with Russ Meyer?

HAJI: I was dancing at a club — I don't remember which one — and someone saw me there, someone who called Russ and said, "There's a Russ Meyer girl here." So he came up to me and asked me to do a reading for a movie he was doing. I told him, "I've never done acting before and I've never considered being an actress. I don't know what to do!" But he told me not to worry, that it was a small part. Fortunately, I was going with a guy at the time who was a fine actor and he coached me through it. I got the part, and I guess it went well; they asked me to come back and read for the lead. I was like, "The lead!" You see, because I didn't get a real education, I couldn't read aloud and all I could think was, "All those lines!"

JEWEL: What movie was this?

HAJI: "Motor Psycho." And after my boyfriend helped me again, I got the lead and it went pretty well. Once Russ got to know me, things worked out

Russ Meyer starlets: Haji, Lori Williams and Tura Satana in "Faster, Pussycat! Kill! Kill!" (1966)

great. He would block everything out and I would stumble through the lines. Then I'd take the script and go memorize it. Meanwhile, everybody else would be like, "Oh, my God, this girl can't read!" But Russ would tell them I was great, then I'd come back and when the camera was moving I'd release all my energy. Ruth Gordon was the same way. She stored her energy until the cameras were rolling.

JEWEL: So your second film with Russ was what?

HAJI: "Faster, Pussycat, Kill! Kill!"

JEWEL: Besides Russ Meyer, were you going out on auditions for other directors?

HAJI: No, because I can't do cold readings. I did get John Cassavetes to let me play in his movie, "Killing of a Chinese Bookie" without a reading...He let us more or less improvise, and he loved my work. I was supposed to work for one day and I ended up working for two weeks. Wouldn't you know it, but that turned out to be his worst movie?

JEWEL: How much of your performance did they keep?

HAJI: Well, when the film trailers started showing around town people called me and said I was going to be a star. The trailers were so great and it looked like I had a big part. But then at the premiere, you could've blinked and missed my part. They cut out all the girls' stuff, which was the best material...still, I think John and Russ were the two men I really enjoyed working with more than anyone. They were real gentlemen and they took their work very seriously, and that's the attitude I have, because I went through the Russ Meyer School of Acting. He's a bull on the set. He doesn't like wimpy women or whiners. I learned so much, and he gave me three leads right in a row!

JEWEL: What was the third movie?

HAJI: "Good Morning and Goodbye!" He had a part for me to ride this broom and live in the woods. It was a great part for me, but he didn't let me do it the way I wanted. He just wanted tits and ass. I wanted to surround myself with animals and spiders and snakes because if you live in the woods, these things are supposed to be your friends. So I borrowed this little boy's snake and shot the scene and when Russ got home, he said, "This bitch is right! But the snake's too small!"

JEWEL: You had quite a costume in that movie!

HAJI: Yes. I glued little ladybugs onto my face. Everything I wore, I got from the woods. I spray-painted maple leaves silver and made my own costumes. I also came up with the title because it seemed like everyone was screwing each other in the film, but they'd always leave first thing in the morning. So I told Russ it was like you'd get up and say "Good morning" and then say "Goodbye!" And he thought it was a good title.

JEWEL: What's your opinion of nudity in film?

HAJI: I stay away from it. Showing a little bit as you're taking something off or putting something on is fine. I have nothing against natural nudity.

JEWEL: What about violence? Do you have anything against that?

HAJI: Well, in real life, there's violence against women. And if you're an actress looking for work, you take just about anything — except, for me, exploitative nudity.

JEWEL: Most people consider Russ Meyer's films as exploitative, but you never went nude in any of his movies, did you?

With Alex Rocco in "Motor Psycho" (1965)

HAJI: No, I didn't want to do nude stuff. I wanted to hold out for the big time! *(laughs)* It's just from my upbringing, I guess. During the movies, I kept up my dancing, but even there, I never danced totally nude.

JEWEL: When did you quit dancing?

HAJI: When everyone went bottomless, that's when I hung up my g-string. I moved to Vegas, but that didn't work out because there was no ocean to play in and no trees to climb. I have to be near nature. Eventually, I got into landscaping and interior design. Fortunately, I have a lot of wealthy friends who let me decorate and landscape their homes.

JEWEL: Is that what you're doing now?

HAJI: Actually, I'm working for Charles Hagen, who's a developer. He builds shopping malls and stuff. I'm his Girl Friday. I organize for him, make sure things are intact. He's not married and he's a very busy man.

JEWEL: Have you ever been married?

HAJI: No, but I love to play house. You don't know how domestic I am. I love the garden, I love to cook...my sister even accused me of being a lesbian. And the truth is, I haven't dated in over a year and a half. It has nothing to do with AIDS, though. It's just that I haven't met anybody! It's so hard to find somebody that turns you on.

JEWEL: Do people recognize you on the streets?

HAJI: Not really. And when they do, it's only because of my nose. But you know, my own nose bothered me. My mother used to say that if you're young and something bothers you, just go to a good plastic surgeon.

JEWEL: What did your family think of your career?

HAJI: My brother was so proud...*(long pause)* but I don't want to talk about him. He died in an accident.

JEWEL: Are you still pursuing acting?

HAJI: Actually, I'm trying to get back into it. I'm just finishing writing a script that features a role for me. I think it's a pretty good script. We'll see.

JEWEL: Were you ever offered porno work?

HAJI: Yes, I was offered all sorts of hard-core but I turned it all down. The only thing I did was a little topless thing for Japan...at least, that's all I remember.

JEWEL: When you look at your films, what do you feel?

HAJI: Sometimes, I think I could've done this better or that different...in that time period, those kinds of films weren't considered in the mainstream. I remember going out on an interview and very proudly telling the casting director I did two films with Russ Meyer. He said, "Oh no, don't put that on your resumé. You won't get a job with that!" I ended up having a big fight with this guy because I had more respect and admiration for Russ at that time...you just can't knock the fact that Russ could take five people out and make a movie for almost no money and one that a lot of people like! *(deep breath)* Another thing about dealing with Russ, he's a professional. You're hired as an actress. You don't have to worry about getting a knock at your door in the middle of the night. That's why Russ is where he is today. He loves the films he makes and he gets the girl who's right for the part, period. Nothing else.

JEWEL: Have you had any close encounters in the casting room?

HAJI: Well, one guy asked me if I wanted to give him "a little head." I said,

"Motor Psycho" (1965)

"I don't want to give you a little head or a lot of head...what I'd like to do is bust your head!" That surprised him because I'm very quiet and people think I'm ignorant. But I told this guy, "You know, I can call you a jerk-off, but the sad thing is there's going to be girls coming in here that will be giving you head and it's truly a shame that there are such stupid girls in this town!"

JEWEL: Do you think that people were given the impression that you were loose and easy because you were one of Russ Meyer's girls?

HAJI: I don't know. I suppose. But I didn't give it much thought...at least, others have been a little more discreet and asked me to be their woman, where they give you the part and take you out to dinner and the whole bit, but still! You can't tell me that the only way to get a part is to put out. I don't care when people tell me something like, "If you want to get anywhere, you're going to have to pay the piper!" I just tell them that their pipe is too little to play!

JEWEL: What would be your ideal role?

HAJI: I want to do a western. I'd like to be a female Clint Eastwood and blow the bad guys away...I'd love to do something Latin, something where I play the congas. I like things very exotic and off the wall.

JEWEL: Do you have a fan club?

HAJI: I've been told I have lots of fans out there, but I don't know. One thing I'd like to do is start selling some nude photos of myself...I like to take pictures of endangered species of animals, then superimpose a picture of me nude, covered in leaves, over the animal. That way it looks like I'm the guardian spirit of the animal. I'd like to sell these to fans and donate the money to saving endangered animals.

JEWEL: If there was anything you could change about your life right now, what would it be?

HAJI: I wish I had received a better education because I want to go into politics. For instance, I'm trying to pass a law that demands all labels indicate where a product has been used in animal research. Like this: They do all sorts of experiments on animals to test the safety of a product. They'll pour gallons of oil down a dog's throat to see how much it takes to kill him! I also want to pass a law that makes available animal birth control. But animal food companies don't want that because it reduces their business.

JEWEL: Are you actively starting programs?

HAJI: Yes, but I'm focusing only on the younger generations. I did some reading on Hitler and do you know that he had the power to convince children to turn in their parents, who would then be executed? That's a tremendous power. I think that the younger generations are the key to the future because the older earthlings don't understand the fairness of life!

"There was this one director, though, who took out a vibrator and chased me around his office."

Kathleen Hughes

Back when the "B" in "B-movies" denoted merely a picture not shot on an "A" budget, the B-movie world had its own stars, drawing down as much fan mail as the biggest box office kings and queens. Kathleen Hughes was and always will be one such star. Though, as she describes below, her occasional voyages into "A" pictures were unsuccessful, she managed to survive the Hollywood studio system and to keep working. And she still keeps working, adding to a career that has spanned more than forty years and continues still.

JEWEL: *(looking over résumé:)* You've really been in Hollywood a long time.

KATHLEEN: I was born in a Hollywood hospital. And I've lived here all my life. You can't be any more Hollywood than that!

JEWEL: What did your parents do?

KATHLEEN: I don't know what my father did. His family was in the rubber business, tires and things. He came to this country primarily to study the rubber businesses here. So he and my mother started off in Akron, Ohio where there's a huge rubber plant. Then gradually moved West. Actually, they came to Hollywood because my uncle, F. Hugh Herbert*, was in the movie business. He was a writer whose credits included: "Scudda Hoo! Scudda Hay!" and "Kiss and Tell." Eventually, the whole family ended up here.

JEWEL: So you went to all local schools?

KATHLEEN: Yes. There was one that I went to called the Progressive School, which I loved. It was right across the street from the Hollywood Bowl. Now there's a parking lot there...I went to Fairfax High, and then to L.A. City College, which is when I was signed by Twentieth-Century Fox.

JEWEL: How did that happen?

KATHLEEN: I had won a scholarship to the Geller acting workshop...See, I had just read an ad in the paper saying that they needed girls to enroll in this drama school so that the G.I.s on the G.I. Bill had girls to act with. It didn't cost me anything. It was a wonderful break. I went to acting classes there while I was going to City College. Eventually I made it into a play called "Night over Taos." Well, I was terrible in it, but I guess I looked good — even though I felt so ill from cramps that I actually passed out after the first act curtain. Well, when they revived me, they said there was talent scout from Fox in the audience.

---

*Not to be confused with character actor Hugh Herbert.

So I made it through the play and this scout got me an audition at Fox. And they signed me! I was about nineteen years old and I got signed to a seven-year contract.

JEWEL: Seven years?

KATHLEEN: But it didn't really mean seven years...and they only paid you 40 out of 52 weeks, so everyone had their salary pro-rated. But it was great, they had their own wonderful drama coach named Helena Serrell. She's still around teaching privately...

JEWEL: What year was this?

KATHLEEN: 1948, I think.

JEWEL: Was there anyone else in your acting class who went on to fame?

KATHLEEN: There was John Derek, whose

name back then was Dare Harris. He was married to Patty Bear, who didn't look anything like any of those clones he's married since then.

JEWEL: So what was your first movie with Fox?

KATHLEEN: "Roadhouse," with Cornel Wilde, Ida Lupino, Celeste Holme and Richard Widmark. I had this scene with Cornel Wilde, who was at the height of his career. I mean, you've never seen anyone so gorgeous in your life. He was to die for...anyway, the scene took place in the bowling alley attached to the roadhouse and I say to Cornel something like, "Make a strike and I'll give you a kiss." And he says, "How could I miss?" Then he bowls a strike. As it turns out, that was the first scene I had cut out of a movie.

JEWEL: What came after "Roadhouse?"

KATHLEEN: "Mother is a Freshman" with Van Johnson and Loretta Young. Now, I'm still in that one...I absolutely loved it.

JEWEL: Now did you get a bonus or anything for making it into a film?

KATHLEEN: Heavens, no. When you're a contract player, you get your salary and that's it. I was making $100 a week, for 40 weeks. So I was getting $4,000 a year. But in 1948, that was good money. Anyway, when my first year was up, they picked up my option and gave me a raise to $125 a week! By the third year, I was up to $150! The next year I wasn't picked up, though.

JEWEL: How did you feel?

KATHLEEN: I was terribly depressed. And I was dropped rather nastily. But I was with a big agency, the Jaffe Agency, which was really big, and they got me all sorts of work...for instance, I got this small part in a sketch for "The Frank Sinatra Show," which was live TV. Anyway, I played the part of this sexy nurse who had the punchline in the sketch. I was so nervous that I garbled the line. It wasn't awful, but it wasn't as funny as it should've been, either. Nonetheless, a producer from Universal was in the audience and came backstage to tell me I should be under contract at Universal. So I got another seven-year contract, which again, didn't mean seven years, really!

JEWEL: Universal was where you made most of your B-movies.

KATHLEEN: Yes. I spent three years there and made six of those films...It started after I had just done a big part in a movie for them. I heard they were doing the first 3-D picture. So I went to the producer and asked to be in it, even though it was only a small role. He tried to talk me out of it, but it was the best career move I ever made. I was later crowned Miss 3-D!

JEWEL: You also did "Cult of the Cobra" at Universal.

KATHLEEN: Oh, it was a really bad experience. I hated the director and he hated me. I guess it was just a bad chemical reaction. The movie was about this magical cobra that gets over to the states and turns into Faith Demure. All I remember was that at the end of the movie, she turned back into a cobra and was about to strike me in my dressing room — I was playing an actress — and I screamed, bringing someone in who throws the cobra out the window. And when it hits the pavement outside, it turns back into a dead Faith Demure.

JEWEL: What was your favorite Universal film?

KATHLEEN: "The Glass Web," with Edward G. Robinson and John Forsythe. I loved that movie. I loved the director and he loved me. And that makes a big difference. Also, Edward G. Robinson was the best kisser in Hollywood. We used to neck in the dressing room.

JEWEL: (laughs) So when did you meet your husband Stanley Rubin?

KATHLEEN: At Universal. I met him at a party, but I just thought he was a dirty old producer. At the time, I was dating Lance Fuller and it was purely platonic, which was all I wanted. I didn't want something complicated. So when Stanley started calling me to date, I wanted nothing to do with him. Several months later, I was in Palm Springs recuperating from a trip to South America, when a girl asked me if I knew Stanley Rubin. "Funny you should ask," I said. "He keeps asking him out." And she thought I was crazy and said he was the nicest man...so I consented to go out with him. *(pause)* When he picked me up, it was like a bolt of lightning hit and I heard bells. I think if he had said, "I don't feel like going out. Let's just go get married," I would have said yes.

JEWEL: So what happened to your career when you did get married?

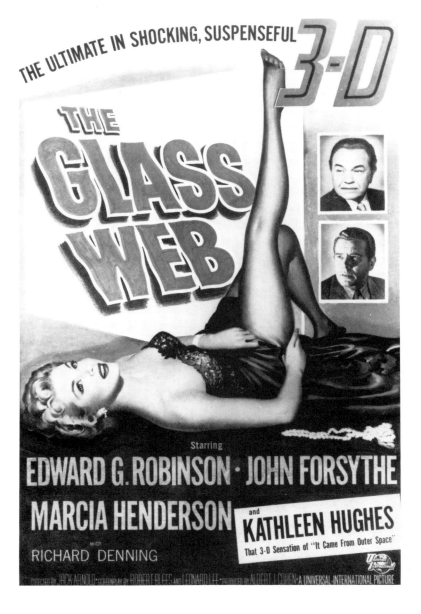

KATHLEEN: It was like I got canned for a wedding present. My contract expired and they didn't renew it.

JEWEL: Do you think it had anything to do with your sudden unavailability?

KATHLEEN: Well...

JEWEL: I mean, I've heard how people like Zanuck and other moguls used to hit on their starlets.

KATHLEEN: Oh, I was never bothered by any of the biggies. There were some directors who would invite me into their office and immediately unzip their pants and start playing with themselves. I don't know what they thought I was going to do! *(laughs)* But never any of the biggies.

JEWEL: *(shocked)* What did you do when this happened?

KATHLEEN: I guess I was too stupid to leave, so I just stood there and watched. I was amazed... one of them had the tiniest little thing, it was hysterical. But it was no big thing. I even ended up working with most of them. There was this one director, though, who took out a vibrator and chased me around his office. I hated him and I would never have worked with him.

JEWEL: What year was this?

KATHLEEN: It was the early fifties. The worst was this Hungarian director who chased me around the room and cornered me. He didn't unzip or anything, but just started banging himself against me, saying, "Oy! Oy! Oy!" Then, about thirty seconds later, he came. I was appalled.

JEWEL: I can imagine!

KATHLEEN: But I'll tell you one funny instance. A director at Paramount asked to see me. But when I found out who it was, I remembered that he had asked to see me while he was at Universal, and he was one of the ones who had whipped it out — and let me tell you, it was as big as a salami. Anyway, I told my agent I would only go see this man if he would go with me. So we get there and the director makes my agent wait in the outer office. When we get inside, sure enough, he whips it out and asks to come in my hand. I didn't have to touch it or anything, he just wanted to come in my hand.

JEWEL: And you let him?

KATHLEEN: Yes, but here's the funny part. After I had it in my hand, I turned and headed for the outer office and he said, "Where are you going?" To which I said, "I'm going to give my agent his ten percent." He was a comedy writer too, you see.

JEWEL: *(laughs)* I sure hope you got a part out this!

KATHLEEN: Yes, we did end up working together. I actually became good friends with him...

JEWEL: I just noticed that on your wall, you have a photo of yourself taken by Tom Kelly.

KATHLEEN: Yes.

JEWEL: Did he tell you that he had done a photo session with Marilyn Monroe, or Norma Jean I guess she was at the time?

KATHLEEN: No. I think I posed for him before Marilyn did. Marilyn and I were contemporaries, you see. In fact, she was Miss Cheesecake of 1951, and I was Miss Cheesecake of 1952. I was a big pin-up queen for the armed forces.

JEWEL: Jumping ahead a few years...What have you done recently?

KATHLEEN: Well, I did "Ironweed." It was funny, my agent called me and asked me how I knew Jack Nicholson. I said I didn't even know him. Well, it turns out that Jack had given my name to casting and wanted me to read for the part of his wife. So on the plane ride back to New York, I read the book the movie was based on. And I didn't think I was right for the part of the wife. But I did like this smaller part of an aging nymphomaniac who had sex in her basement with the junk man. I loved that part, and when I went in to meet the director, Hector Babenco, it was one of those things where we hit it off right off the bat. He let me audition for the part. Three weeks later I got this call from someone asking for my measurements. I said, "You mean I got the part?" And she said, "You mean your agent didn't tell you?" *(laughs)* But, of course, I got cut out of that picture, too.

JEWEL: You must've been so disappointed.

KATHLEEN: I was, but it was so much fun working on that film, working with Jack Nicholson. They even let us all watch dailies, and I remember watching our scene and it was so funny, we even got applause from everyone in there. The author of the book even liked it!

JEWEL: Now you were also cut out of your husband's latest film, "Revenge," weren't you?

KATHLEEN: Yes, and I'd always wanted to play a nun. I researched the role and everything...but again, the film came in forty-five minutes too long. Still, I have my footage on videotape.

JEWEL: You were cut out of "The Couch Trip" too? Didn't that drive you crazy?

KATHLEEN: Yes, but you can't dwell on it. You would drive yourself crazy. I try to keep a very healthy outlook.

JEWEL: Did you ever get scared as you got older, thinking that there wouldn't be any parts left for you?

KATHLEEN: There will always be parts for older people. Maybe not the leads, but parts. And I feel like I was part of the Golden Age of Hollywood. I traveled all over the world and I will have movies that live forever. I don't mind getting older.

JEWEL: Do you still receive fan mail?

KATHLEEN: Oh, yes. I've received carloads of fan mail. I try to write every one of them back. If I don't, I feel so guilty...I don't know how they actually find me, but I guess our address is listed in Hollywood's "Who's Who?" So that must be how.

JEWEL: Does it worry you, considering what happened to Rebecca Schaeffer, who was murdered recently by a psychotic fan?

KATHLEEN: Oh, I'm not worried. No one would want to kill me. Plus, we have an extensive burglar alarm here. And none of my fan mail has been anything but sweet.

JEWEL: Did you ever do any nudity in any of your films?

KATHLEEN: There was a movie called "The Big Brawl," a kung fu movie, where they needed a quick scene with a middle-aged couple in bed. So I got the part without even auditioning, but I was real nervous about it. I kept wondering if they were going to like my breasts. Anyway, they flew me all the way to San Antonio — first-class, mind you — and after I was all in make-up and costume, the director said he'd been thinking about it and he can't use the scene. So they sent me home. And I'm thinking, "Oh, there must be a God."

JEWEL: But what's your attitude towards nudity in film?

KATHLEEN: If it's tasteful, a few frames maybe, that's fine. But I've seen movies that really offend me. Stuff where there's a couple lying in bed and she could have very easily had the sheet up over her!

JEWEL: What about violence? What's your opinion of screen violence?

KATHLEEN: I hate it. I think that people see it on the screen and go out and copy it.

JEWEL: If there was one thing you could change about this world, what would it be?

KATHLEEN: I think that the world is going to come to an end because of over population. I'm a nut about it...I'm very active in the Pro-Choice movement.

JEWEL: Is there anything you would like to change about your own life?

KATHLEEN: I feel so lucky...I suppose that if there's one thing I could do differently, it would've been to have take classes earlier in my life.

48

"I didn't know karate very well, so the producers told me to practice in the aisle on the plane ride over."

Jillian Kesner

Probably the most athletic of all the actresses in this book, Jillian Kesner is a good example of making your skills work for you. In recent years, with a rage for Kung Fu films starring men such as Chuck Norris, Bruce Lee and dozens of men claiming the mantle of "Bruce Lee's hand-picked successor," it was inevitable that someone should seek out the female equivalent. When that happened, Jillian was there with the physical prowess needed. And, when it wasn't happening, she has had the business acumen to invest in other areas.

JEWEL: So you were born in Portsmouth, Virginia?

JILLIAN: Yeah, but my father was in the Navy so we moved all over the U.S.. I went to high school in Denver, then to the University of Colorado, where I studied business. I never wanted to be an actress. I never even thought of it until I took this vacation to Southern California. All I had to see was the San Bernadino Valley and I knew this was where I wanted to live. But my parents made me finish up my degree first.

JEWEL: Did you get along with your parents?

JILLIAN: I loved my parents, but I've always been quite independent. My mother likes to tell me how when I was ten, if I didn't get my way I'd bang my head against the door until I passed out. I always wanted to do things my own way. My father died while I was in college, but we had a good relationship. Of the three girls in my family, I was most like a boy! *(laughs)* So my dad would come to my horse shows and watch like I was an athlete or something...I needed some way to express myself, something to be obsessive about, and horses gave me something to really care about. We were all brought up as over-achievers.

JEWEL: When did you realize you were more than just a tomboy?

JILLIAN: I won this contest. They voted for prettiest girl in school, you know? And I won. All I could think was "What? Me? Why would I win that?" Then I came to like getting all the attention and I realized maybe I could use this *(laughs, indicates her body)* but I never thought of acting. I just thought maybe I could win a few more contests.

JEWEL: Did you join a sorority in college?

JILLIAN: My sister was in a sorority and I was pressured into joining and being a goody-goody and excelling like I did in high school, but for some reason I rejected it completely.

JEWEL: Did that have anything to do with the Vietnam War and the sentiments of the time?

JILLIAN: Actually, the hippie thing was going out about then, but I was hanging around people who did rather...rebellious things. Non-sorority type things.

JEWEL: Did you do drugs?

JILLIAN: Yes! *(laughs)* Everybody did. LSD, all of that.

JEWEL: So after you got your degree, you came out to Los Angeles?

JILLIAN: Yeah, I lived with Lance Rentzel. He was my first real boyfriend. He played football for the Rams and the Dallas Cowboys. We almost got married.

JEWEL: How did you meet Lance?

JILLIAN: When I first got here, I lived with my sister in a single on Palm Drive in Beverly Hills. The whole place was the size of a normal kitchen. Anyway, we were driving down the street one day and met these people who invited us to some tennis tournament at Bill Cosby's house. That's where I met Lance. He was always invited to all these parties with celebrities, which was really fun, meeting all these glamorous people, but I still didn't think about being an actress.

JEWEL: So how did you finally get in front of a camera?

JILLIAN: I can't exactly remember...I think it was Lance who said to go interview with this commercial agent he knew. So I got this print ad work through a guy named Johnny Mango. My biggest ad was for Tahitian Tan. I had billboards all over L.A..

JEWEL: Did you tell all your friends?

JILLIAN: Yeah, I was so proud. It seemed like a dream. See, when you're growing up in Denver, it never dawns on you that you could move to L.A. and do what I was doing. My mother certainly never encouraged me to do it. In fact, she still complains that I picked the hardest profession there is. She wanted me to use my brain and my business degree but I just felt like hanging out in Southern California and seeing what happened.

JEWEL: What did happen after the Tahitian Tan ad?

JILLIAN: I did a bunch of car ads, make-up ads, shampoo, bicycles, bathing suits...everything. My first big acting job was on "Happy Days." I played Henry Winkler's girl friend and it was so hard being in front of a live audience. I had no experience doing real acting and all of a sudden I'm, you know, acting! *(laughs)*

JEWEL: So you'd never done any theatre?

JILLIAN: Right at the same time, Evan Lester, chairman of the Civic Light Opera, hired me for a musical comedy called "Wonderful Town." At the time, that was the best training I possibly could have has as an actress. It's a really funny story how I got the part, too. I auditioned up in San Francisco where the play was running at the Kern Theatre and I said, "Is this supposed to be funny?" Well, it's a comedy, you know, based on this 1935 play called "My Sister Eileen." Really kinda corny humor. Anyway, I asked if this play was supposed to be funny in front of twenty-five people. Well, everybody put their heads down because it was an insult to them. But Evan loved me. He thought it was great, so I read for the part and was probably terrible but he hired me, anyway. I don't know if he tells everyone this but he said to me, "You're gonna be the Sarah Bernhardt of the future."

JEWEL: Let's hear about your first feature.

JILLIAN: After starting out classy, at the Music Center and on "Happy Days," I interviewed for a part in "The Student Body" and got the lead role. In fact, there's a scene in the movie where I throw this ashtray 'cause I'm going crazy. Well, the scene ended up in the movie "The Thin Blue Line" because the guys in that film were watching "The Student Body" at the drive-in right before the cop gets killed.

JEWEL: Does that make you think about what films you're going to choose from now on?

JILLIAN: Well, "The Thin Blue Line" was a well-respected movie. It was the critic's choice of 1988. I don't really feel responsible for what happened. In fact, it made me feel kind of neat. I felt really proud.

JEWEL: Really proud?

JILLIAN: You know what I mean. Proud that I'm in that movie. It makes me feel like the things we do, these B-movies, have an impact on people.

JEWEL: Are there some kinds of movies you won't do?

JILLIAN: There are some things I won't do in a movie. Like too many sexual things.

JEWEL: What about "Jaded?" That was pretty...

JILLIAN: Well, let me explain about "Jaded." The director was Yugoslavian. She lived with Orson Welles for twenty years or whatever and she thinks nothing of taking off her clothes. I knew going into the project that it would have that European feel, like "The Unbearable Lightness of Being." Of course, that was a class act picture and "Jaded" was a low-life picture about the low-life of Venice.

JEWEL: But in that movie you—

JILLIAN: There's different types of sexual...like "The Big Easy," what Ellen Barkin does. I think that's okay, if it's done tastefully. The rape scene in "Jaded" was very violent. I almost didn't do it, but I knew how important it was...can we come back to this?

JEWEL: So how do you feel about violence towards women?

JILLIAN: I feel terrible about it.

JEWEL: But it won't stop you from doing a movie?

JILLIAN: I don't mean to be defensive about "Jaded," it's just that it falls into a special category of film. It'll never be popular in the U.S.

JEWEL: Aside from European films then, what's your limit?

JILLIAN: I wouldn't let them just cut me up naked.

JEWEL: Okay, say your character's going to get slashed through the chest and they want you to do it topless?

JILLIAN: I wouldn't want to do it. But I'd talk to the director like I do in every film. Like in "Jaded," I refused at first to do the rape scene. But the director told me she'd take off all her clothes and double for me. She'd done that kind of thing in any of Orson Welles' movies, the ones he made later on. So when she offered to do that and explained the humor of the scene, how the two guys were afraid to fight each unless they had me in the middle, I felt different. I think if there's a reason and meaning to nudity, I'm much more open to it.

JEWEL: Let's talk about your karate pictures...

JILLIAN: This is the best. The first one was the most exciting experience of my life. It's called "Firecracker." My agent called and told me to get over to see Roger Corman, who's famous for discovering people. It was just magical. Anyway, I was replacing someone already cast, so I found out in twenty-four hours that I had to fly to Manila. Well, I didn't know karate very well, so the producers told me to practice in the aisle on the plane ride over *(laughs)*. I'm not kidding! And once I got there, I was just blown away. The conditions were horrible. It was so humid. One time, we were in the jungle and I looked down and saw this eight inch roach. I just couldn't believe it. I mean, I'm staying in this five-star hotel and I walk out the door and I'm in the jungle!

JEWEL: Did the film have technical advisors?

JILLIAN: Absolutely. There was a Bruce Lee type guy named Raymond King. He was my trainer. Without that guy, I'm telling you, I would've looked ridiculous. Even so, anyone who knows karate can tell from looking at the film that I'm no black belt. Although I do have a blue belt in Tong Su Do and a purple belt in Shodokan...

JEWEL: You've done other karate pictures too, haven't you?

JILLIAN: It's funny, on one I worked with all the famous Filipino actors and Darby Hinton was the male lead. Then eight months later, I worked with Ed Murphy and Hope Holiday on "Raw Force."

JEWEL: Do fans ever write you?

JILLIAN: Sure. Sometimes they even write weird kind of letters that say, "I put up your picture and dream about you." Very intensely obsessive stuff.

JEWEL: Have any of these obsessed fans ever taken it a step further than a letter?

JILLIAN: No, nothing like that. Thank God.

JEWEL: Has your mother seen your movies?

JILLIAN: Yes, but...my sister has. They're proud of me as an actress but I don't think they like any of the nudity. I think they're a little conservative, kind of old-fashioned.

JEWEL: What do you see yourself doing in five or ten years?

JILLIAN: Well, I quit the entertainment business three years ago. I have a real estate license now. I own a business in Las Vegas, part of a shopping center and a home. I'm a businesswoman now. I'd never be able to survive if acting was my only thing. But I came back to acting recently when Gary Graver called and said, "I'm gonna do a film called 'Moon in Scorpio' and I'm gonna write a part especially for you. Are you interested?" The timing was right so I thought, why not? My attitude was a little better then, too. I wasn't as depressed and disillusioned with the business as when I quit. A lot of those dreams you have when you're first starting, they're a little unrealistic *(laughs)*. It doesn't always happen like with Farrah Fawcett, whom I worked with once.

JEWEL: Actually, Farrah worked for twelve years before she got onto "Charlie's Angels."

JILLIAN: Really? Well, I did one of my first jobs with her; we both played beauty contestants...she won, though.

JEWEL: Will you still take off your clothes?

JILLIAN: I'd rather not do it in every movie, but I don't mind. I don't think it's a bad thing at all. I've never done *Playboy*, but I'm certainly not against it.

JEWEL: Ever had a nightmare interview?

JILLIAN: I had a guy who, I was told, was a casting person, but he wasn't. He tried to make me play a scene with him where he laid down on the couch and closed his eyes and said, "Pretend like I'm gay and you're trying to convince me *(laughs)*, you know, to be heterosexual." I knew what he was getting at but I didn't do the scene the way he wanted.

JEWEL: Who else have you worked with that went on to become famous?

JILLIAN: Robin Williams and...my first commercial was with Tom Selleck. It was for Ultra-Ban deodorant. That's a funny one. He's a great guy, but I knew that he was married. It was totally professional. I didn't try to come on.

JEWEL: When you are alone, how do you pass the time?

JILLIAN: I do some reading on mostly spiritual things that relate to man's place in the universe and my place in the universe. I like to consider how I can be a better person and how the world can be a better place, because I really expected much more...but I know one person can't do it all. When I finally decided to be an actress, I was so young...but I thought I could contribute a lot in films by portraying important people. But it hasn't turned out like that at all, has it? I'm not saying I still don't have those aspirations, but I know this interview, this book is about low-budget movies for the most part...so let's get real.

"Firecracker" (1981)

"My mom...has these group prayer meetings and they sit there praying that I'm not going to be a bimbo anymore."

Becky LeBeau

If there is a physical "look" to which a B-movie actress is expected to conform, Becky LeBeau probably comes closer than anyone working today. The blonde and busty "bimbo" stereotype can be cruel...but when one can make it work for themselves, as Becky has, it can be profitable. Becky has that look and has learned to make it work for herself; she is not exaggerating one bit when she speaks of her legions of fans racing to buy her posters, videos and photos. They know her from her appearances in the pages of *Playboy* and attendant cable programming; on one recent night, she appeared in each of five shows aired on The Playboy Channel and in two fillers between these programs. One of these shows — her "Soft Bodies Invitational" for which she is producer, star and musical director — is a good example of how a bit of business acumen, coupled with a fan following, can pay off. Several other actresses are now looking to follow Becky's lead...and not just for financial reasons. Exploitation films, after all, have been know to exploit those on the screen, as well as those in the audience. In this business, where the biggest bucks are usually made by those who hire, not those the fans pay to see, it is nice to see that Becky has seized both opportunities.

Becky is most often cast as a blonde bimbo and/or stripper. She was the girl in the hot tub with Rodney Dangerfield in "Back to School" and her other film titles include "He's My Girl," "The Underachievers," "Transylvania Twist," "Not Of This Earth," "Rock-A-Die Baby," "Joysticks," "School Spirit" and "Taking It All Off." She still gets recognized from her appearances in David Lee Roth's videos of "California Girls" and "Just a Gigolo."

JEWEL: So you're a Los Angeles native?

BECKY: I was born in Beverly Hills. My parents still live here. I went to Beverly Hills High, then I went to U.S.C. and graduated in 1986, although I'm not in the yearbook and I don't know why. I was a psychology major...*(giggles)* with a music minor! I have a bachelor's degree. I'm not really dumb. *(laughs)* I just act it!

JEWEL: What's the rest of your family like?

BECKY: I have a brother named Michael LeBeau. That's our real name by the way for all you out there! *(laughs)* He's younger than me...I won't say my age, but I'm not thirty yet. My dad's an electrical engineer. My mom was a substitute teacher, but now she's into dogs. She takes care of them and feeds them. She's a born-again Christian and she's really into it, you know? It's kinda weird.

JEWEL: Were you popular in school?

BECKY: I was a pretty good student scholastically, I mean like A's and B's and maybe a "C" every now and then...but everybody called me "Retard" because I was really bad in sports, and being good in sports is really important when you're a kid. I couldn't care less about sports, but it made me unpopular.

JEWEL: I'll bet you went to school with a lot of famous people.

BECKY: Sean Cassidy was one year ahead of me. Jamie Lee Curtis was in my drama class. William Shatner's daughter, Leslie, was in my P.E. class.

JEWEL: When did you realize that you were attractive?

BECKY: I was always really awkward and kinda chubby. Then one summer in high school, I just kind of blossomed. I didn't know I was good-looking until my boobs got big in my junior year and then the guys started, you know...I got a lot of attention. *(laughs)*

JEWEL: Did you date a lot after that?

BECKY: Yeah, but I was a real tease. I liked having boyfriends, but I didn't want to sleep with them, so they called me names like "Pricktease" and then they lied and said I was a slut. I guess it's because I would flirt with them and go out on dates and maybe fool around a little, but I wouldn't sleep with them. I wasn't ready for that! So by the time I was in my senior year, word was around about me and I didn't have as many dates.

JEWEL: Does anybody you grew up with ever recognize you from the Playboy Channel? And are they shocked?

BECKY: I don't know! I guess...actually I'm kinda embarrassed because you just don't know where people are coming from. It would be nice to say I was in some big movie instead...

JEWEL: Well, "Back to School" was —

BECKY: That's actually the only big movie I've been in. I've done some TV stuff and some commercials that run all the time, but otherwise it's just bimbo stuff or topless stuff, which is fine. I don't mind it.

JEWEL: You don't mind people considering you a bimbo?

BECKY: Oh no...this is my philosophy: Since I'm not the greatest actress in the world, if you give me something really hard to do, it's really hard for me...I'm much better at comedy and I happen to be good at being a bimbo! *(laughs)*

JEWEL: Wait a minute, weren't you a psychology major?

BECKY: It doesn't matter. I know in my heart that I'm intelligent. I run a business...you know, there's so many things that I do besides acting. I'm a musician and a songwriter. I know I'm not dumb. I don't care if I'm playing a bimbo. I think it's funny, it's cute. *(giggles)* When I did that B-movie pictorial for *Playboy*, one of the girls, Monique Gabrielle, called me up and wanted me to go out on the talk show circuit and talk about how they're calling us bimbos. But I couldn't because *Playboy* sells my videos. It's like biting the hand that feeds! Secondly, I can't see myself complaining about being called a bimbo because I'm not insecure about it! I'm not Meryl Streep or something...I mean, I love acting, but I'm just not as serious about it as other people. That's a bad word. I am very serious, but I'm not serious about being a serious actress, you know? *(laughs)*

JEWEL: So when was the first time you were in front of a camera and you got that urge to be an actress?

BECKY: When I was little, my mom would take us to the Santa Monica Pier four times a week. Well, there were those machines you put money in and get a picture. I'd spend about ten dollars of my mom's money taking pictures. I

was so into it! My hair was all wet and scraggly but even then I was photogenic in stills...on screen I've never really seen myself look good, except in maybe one called "Taking It All Off."

JEWEL: I thought you looked great in "The Underachievers."

BECKY: I looked okay in that one. But in all the other stuff, like "Not of This Earth," I looked horrible. And "Transylvania Twist," this new one by Concorde/Horizon that I'm in, I looked stupid.

JEWEL: How did you feel about working with Traci Lords?

BECKY: When I first found out I was going to be in "Not of This Earth," they were keeping the leads a secret. I've done stuff with porn stars before for Playboy and Electric Blue, but they weren't porn shows. I don't really like being associated with that realm so, when I found out Traci was in the picture, I wasn't too happy about it. But once the film was out and I saw how she was accepted, I didn't feel bad anymore (laughs).

JEWEL: Let's get back to the first time you were in front of a camera... professionally...

BECKY: This is interesting. There's a radio station that used to be in Los Angeles called KMET. And in '82, there was this song by J. Geils called "Angel in the Centerfold." They were doing some promotion with the Playboy Channel and having a centerfold contest. So my boyfriend, who I've been dating almost nine years — it took eight years to get engaged (shows ring)...I had it made for me. (Jewel "oohs" and "aahs") — anyway, he was trying to convince me to enter, but I always thought those girls in *Playboy* were sluts and it was like, "Psst, c'mere, let me take your picture." And then you go in some dark alley, you know? But I had the wrong impression. They really treat you wonderful, like a queen. So he convinced me to turn in some pictures that weren't nude. I was ten or fifteen pounds heavier then, wearing this tied-up shirt and these stupid little shorts and there were a thousand entries but guess who won? I was so excited! I'd never won anything in my life, and mine wasn't even nude!

JEWEL: What did you win?

BECKY: A trip to a J. Geils concert and a *Playboy* test. I didn't get to be a Playmate 'cause I was kind of heavy. But I walked in there and I'd never taken off my clothes and so I was in this teddy taking pictures when [photographer] Ken Marcus says, "That looks terrible! Get naked!" (laughs) After about thirty seconds, I was fine, just walking around naked. I didn't care! (laughs)

JEWEL: What was your first real acting job?

BECKY: It was "Joysticks" in '83. That was my S.A.G. card film*. I had to sort of tease this guy at a hot dog stand who was holding a hot dog and it slips out and goes down my blouse.

JEWEL: Are you satisfied with the money you've been paid?

BECKY: No, because now that I'm behind the camera and producing my own stuff, I can see how girls can get exploited. I think that the money isn't enough, you should be getting more, especially for doing sexy topless stuff.

JEWEL: Because it can come back to haunt you.

---

* *Screen Actors Guild. In order to join S.A.G., you need to get work on one — sometimes two — TV shows or movies covered by the S.A.G. contract. Most low-budget films are non-S.A.G., thereby accounting for the tendency of some to pay poorly (if at all) and to not treat actors well.*

BECKY: That's the thing about being a club stripper...people forget. But with film and video, it's around forever.

JEWEL: How did you get into producing your own videos?

BECKY: I'd been doing a lot of videos, sexy T-and-A stuff, without releases, just for private people. Mostly they're just putting on girdles and taking off girdles, little scenarios, talking to yourself...hardly any editing. I've done two breast battles. *(laughs)* You know what a breast battle is?

JEWEL: No! *(laughs)*

BECKY: It's when me and another girl go, "My boobs are bigger than yours! I'll show you!" Then you like bang your boobs together. *(laughs)* There's also these exercises where you rub your boobs to the side and people make an hour videotape of you with no editing.

JEWEL: And this is mail order?

BECKY: Actually, the one I'm thinking of, a private person puts up a couple thousand dollars, whatever it takes to pay everyone. This one particular man wanted to be there for the shoot so he told his wife in Idaho or wherever that he was going on a fishing trip to California. *(laughs)* If we pretended we were really mad at each other while we're having this breast battle, we got an extra hundred dollar tip at the end of the day. So the whole time we had to say to each other, "I'll get you in the next round!"

JEWEL: And this guy from Idaho's sitting there, watching the whole thing?

BECKY: Just watching; then they gave the tape to him.

JEWEL: So it's just for his own amusement?

BECKY: Oh, yeah...I've done a couple tapes for private parties like that, but the mail order people, you get through mail lists. I put ads in some men's magazines and they send me a check or money order. They're $19.95 for a half hour.

JEWEL: How many units have you sold?

BECKY: By myself, probably 800. *Playboy* sells a lot more than that, but my store distributor isn't doing that well.

JEWEL: Where did you ever get the idea for this?

BECKY: There was this one man who produced this "Becky Bubbles" video, which was just thirty minutes of me swimming around topless in a pool. Then I'd go lay in the sun with these two other girls and swing on the backyard tree. I mean, really doing nothing. Then at the end, I blow-dry my hair, put on nail polish and wave goodbye. He made a lot of money off that tape because of me. I was his best selling tape, and that gave me the idea. So I wrote this script called "Calling all Bimbos" and rented equipment and everything and hired all these girls and tried to direct and...it was just awful. But I still had the equipment and I got this idea to shoot some sexy stuff like I do for everyone else. So I had Steve's friend come over and I did this little French maid thing where I rubbed my boobs all over him *(laughs)* Then we shot a bunch of other stuff like me in a Jacuzzi and me washing a car in the sun.

JEWEL: This was on 3/4 inch tape?

BECKY: It's too expensive on film. Plus, with video, you can see what you're getting. I also do all the music because I've been a songwriter since I was twelve. I've been in a bunch of rock bands. I play piano and guitar.

JEWEL: How did Playboy come into the picture?

BECKY: I submitted it to a lot of TV channels and Playboy actually licensed it. It's called "Soft Bodies."

JEWEL: What exactly does "Soft Body" mean?

BECKY: It means no plastic, no plastic surgery. It's my little gimmick. I figure 90% of the girls in this town have boob jobs. I think guys want to see girls who are natural.

JEWEL: Let me ask about your fans...

BECKY: Well, I sell photos in the mail. I try not to send letters back except, well, this one guy sent me a letter and he's crippled. He's got some bone disease, so I write him back. I also market nude photos of myself to my fans. I have a flyer advertising a set of 8x10s and there are photo sets in four different locations. These guys write in — most of them are illiterate, I can barely read what they write — and it doesn't make sense because they could go to a newsstand and buy a men's magazine with tons of nude girls. But I guess they want to buy something personal. See, I write on the flyer that these are one time only, exclusive photos from my private portfolio. Then I write something on the photos like, "I'm a born exhibitionist and I decided to catch myself in one of these moments for you."

JEWEL: Ever get any obsessive or weird fans?

BECKY: This one guy from Greenville, South Carolina, got my number from S.A.G. and called up and goes, "Becky? Is this Becky? I don't believe it!" He was really sweet but he kept calling and calling. He wanted to preside over my fan club, nothing threatening. But the next time he called, I said, "No, this isn't Becky. This is her sister. Becky's married." Then he said, "You sure sound like Becky." So I said, "Well, we sound alike, but we don't look alike. She got the looks and I got the brains! *(laughs)*"

JEWEL: What does your family think about your career?

BECKY: My mom prays for me. She kind of blocks what I do out of her mind and prays for me. She has these group prayer meetings and they sit there praying that I'm not going to be a bimbo anymore.

JEWEL: And your father?

BECKY: He got mad because his friend saw me in *Playboy*, but he said he never saw me.

JEWEL: How do you feel about sex and violence in films?

BECKY: I've never done a sex scene in a movie. There was some Al Pacino movie where they wanted me in bed with him, and even though he was famous, I turned it down. I try to keep my image light, the person no one ever gets. I've done nudity and I don't really think twice about it, but you have to draw the line.

JEWEL: What about violence, being violated as a woman?

BECKY: I'm against that. If you're talking about slasher movies where a pretty woman is violated or raped, I know there are studies that show a direct correlation between the movies and real life violence. But I don't think looking at nudity in magazines...I don't think they've been able to draw any connection between that and...

JEWEL: So you wouldn't do a violent movie?

BECKY: I'd feel really strange about it. About a month ago, though, Julia Parton and I were in this bondage video. We were playing chess and this girl was tied up on the bed behind us. It was really stupid, but I did think about the moral implications of this.

JEWEL: Have you ever had a less than memorable interview?

BECKY: I have those all the time! *(laughs)* I remember, I went in for this one recently and I didn't want the part because the casting guy only wanted to give me a nude part, so I said forget it. Then he said, "Well, can you model for us? We haven't seen your body in a few years." I was acting like I didn't know what he meant. I had on this tight dress and I knew he just wanted me to take off my clothes, so I told him I had a bikini down in the car. He just goes, "Oh, you don't need a bikini." Then I said, "Oh, you just want me to take my clothes off?" I mean, why didn't he just say so? *(laughs)*

JEWEL: How do you feel about getting older and playing these parts?

BECKY: It's kinda weird...I always feel too old inside. It's not like anyone says "You look too old for the part!" But I think about that all the time. I wonder when I'm going to wake up one morning and...

JEWEL: Do you think you and Steve will have kids right after you're married?

BECKY: Well, we don't really like kids. And I don't want to ruin my body right now, you know. I don't have any maternal instincts, but I do love puppies. I just haven't gotten to the baby phase yet. They kind of, like, gross me out! *(laughs)* I know that sounds immature, but probably what's going to happen is I'll be 45 or so and it'll be too late.

JEWEL: Has there been any one person who's influenced your career?

BECKY: I liked Suzanne Somers on "Three's Company," and I would've loved to have that part. I guess I admire her, too. The thing I don't like about her acting, though, is I don't like people who try to copy others and she tries to do the Marilyn Monroe thing with the little lisp and all.

JEWEL: How do you feel about yourself right now?

BECKY: I feel good about myself. I'm not a sex bomb. I just look sexy and can act sexy for a camera. But I'm not frigid or anything, either! *(laughs)* I'm just a regular girl, but some people think I'm a sex maniac. This one guy wanted to buy my video and I was trying to get the price higher, saying "I've got a very nice box," and he says, "I'll bet you do!" I get comments like this all the time. There are some videos I've done that I wish weren't out there. When you do them it isn't so bad, but they turn out so darn sleazy looking!

"I can't stand the fact that I let myself be manipulated by any schmuck."

Lisa London

I first met Lisa London in an acting class about five years ago. I was immediately impressed with her persistence...her determination to never allow a door to be slammed in her face. Five years later, she is still that way, still focussing on getting that next play or that next movie. Of all the actresses in this book, Lisa is the one I would I pick as "Least Likely to be Stopped." In a business where being discouraged can be an everyday occurrence, that can be an important asset.

JEWEL: You were raised in this area, weren't you?

LISA: I was born in Santa Monica but I was raised in Palm Springs. My father was from the South side of Chicago and my mother was from the Bronx, so they wanted to raise a family in a very mellow, normal environment. My father owned a radio station in Palm Springs. My mother was a model...she could've done anything, she was so gorgeous, but she gave up everything to marry my father and raise four kids. Now my father owns some Indian Bingo parlors in Arizona.

JEWEL: So you went to the famous Palm Springs high school?

LISA: Also known as "Palm Springs Country Club." I got straight A's and I ditched school almost every day...but I knew from the second I was born what I wanted to do so my education didn't matter. I wanted to act. In fact, there are home movies of me when I was three years old as "The Little Tyrant," running the whole family.

JEWEL: Were you popular as a child?

LISA: I was a very strange kid. I was popular in the sense that everyone wanted to be around me and be my friend. I was very precocious, though. I even started "Lisa London's Most Popular Girl's Club" in sixth grade. But I had a very definite ugly duckling stage and I'd find these letters that my friends wrote to each other saying "Can you believe Joe Blow likes Lisa? She's so ugly." That really tore me up. But it also made me realize that the most important parts of you are your wit and your talent.

JEWEL: When did you realize you weren't ugly?

LISA: I still think I'm ugly. It's very strange...sometimes I can look in the mirror and think, "Okay, this person looks all right." But deep down inside I don't really think so.

JEWEL: When did you start dating?

LISA: My first real boyfriend was Joe Namath. I was sixteen and he was thirty at the time. See, I never really liked anyone my own age.

JEWEL: *(laughs)* How in the world did you meet Joe Namath?

LISA: I met him at this Pro-Am golf tournament that my father was the head of. It's really funny, because no one had ever asked me out before then. But Joe's the one who really got me my break in acting...He was taping a show called "The Waverly Wonders," something I'm sure is on everyone's top ten list. Anyway, his agent at the time was Mike Greenfield, who probably thought, "I'll get into this little brat's pants if I get her a small part in something," but I got the lead in "H.O.T.S."

JEWEL: *(surprised)* Did you even have a S.A.G. card?

LISA: No, and I'd never even studied acting. I'd done my own plays and stuff since I was a kid, but I had no training whatsoever. I had no credits.

JEWEL: "H.O.T.S." is kind of a cult classic...what does it stand for?

LISA: Actually, it was four girls' names: Honey, O'Hara, Teri and Sam. I was O'Hara. We had formed this kind of sorority because we couldn't get into any others, which is kind of ironic because that was how it was for me, always kind of the outsider. The other weird thing was that my idol has always been Scarlet O'Hara and there I was playing this part.

JEWEL: Who else was in that movie with you?

LISA: Susan Kiger, Pamela Bryant, K.C. Winkler and Lindsay Bloom...It's funny, there's this one scene where I go up in a hot air balloon, and why they had me go up with the stunt people is beyond my comprehension because all you see in the shot is this little dot in the balloon. Anyway, the worst part was, to land a hot air balloon you literally have to crash. Well, we're out in Thousand Oaks, hovering above sheep herding country and the stuntman goes green. Next thing I know, we crash into these bushes and we're all cut from head to toe. Then this guy comes up on a horse and we think we're rescued, but he's Mexican and doesn't speak English. And he thinks we're total freaks because I'm in a bikini and one of the stuntmen's in a bear suit and another's dressed as a girl. So when we got back to the set, all they wanted to know was "Is the balloon okay?" I learned a very valuable lesson about filmmaking from that one. *(laughs)*

JEWEL: What did you do after "H.O.T.S."?

LISA: The director of that movie, Gerald Cindel, had taken the film over to William Morris' literary department and I got this call from someone who turned out to be the cousin of one my best friends. I guess he called because he thought I had a great look...a great pair of looks, right? *(laughs)* Anyway, William Morris signed me and assigned me to Peter Myers, who was wonderful. He believed in me 110% and got me "The Happy Hooker Goes to Hollywood," which was pretty good for a girl who'd never done anything, to star in two movies back to back. That movie was another incredible learning experience...It's about a bunch of prostitutes who want to make a movie and outsmart the big studios. I worked with some wonderful actors, Phil Silvers and Richard Deacon, who are both dead now. But I also learned that I really did have a gift for comedy, which I'd always taken for granted. But that's so important, to be able to make people laugh.

JEWEL: Do you have any funny memories of that film?

LISA: Oh God, yes...We were filming at the Ambassador Hotel and everyone that worked there actually thought we were real hookers and, you know...*(laughs)* so of course, we played it up to the hilt.

JEWEL: Any hidden talents?

LISA: I write poetry and I'd love to write screenplays.

JEWEL: You sing, too, don't you?

LISA: I've always sung but, like acting, I've never had any real experience. But I was in a group called "The Pin-Ups" for CBS Records. It was the most incredible good-luck story ever...I did this calendar shoot for Harley-Davidson and they were months late on my check. So my girlfriend and I were sitting around the pool drinking shots of tequila and I'm going, "Goddamit, I want that check!" And my girlfriend goes, "Let's just go get it!" Well, I'll do anything after a few shots of tequila, so we went over to their offices on Sunset looking like total freaks in shorts and cowboys boots — before that was even in style. Anyway, we're banging on the office door and no one's answering. Finally this little man sticks his head out of the office door across the hall and says (in this funny accent) "Excuz me, Miz, but do you sing?" And for some reason I said I've been singing for years." Anyway, I got an audition for this white version of the Pointer Sisters that CBS was putting together.

JEWEL: And..?

LISA: It was horrible. I thought I was abominable. So I went to Las Cabos the next day thinking there was no way I would get this thing, but I get this call from my boyfriend who says I got the part and CBS is sending over contracts. Well, it turns out that there was this international talent search for this group, and I got the lead vocals. We did phenomenally well in Europe, we even had a number one record in Germany called "Song on the Radio." And when the Lakers won that championship in '82 or '83, I don't remember, they used this other song of ours called "Just about a Dream." After that, we did every show over here from Merv Griffin to "Dance Fever."

JEWEL: Why did you break up?

LISA: When it came time for CBS to renew our option they only wanted two of us, and we'd become really close. Plus we were really burned-out...not to mention that I'd just been offered my first dramatic part, in "Sudden Impact."

JEWEL: With Clint Eastwood?

LISA: Yeah...I'm the set-up for this guy they want you to hate, this murderer-rapist guy. And I'm supposed to draw out sympathy for this prostitute I'm playing so you really hate this guy's guts when he totally brutalizes her. But the funny thing is, people would talk to me about this part and say how much they hated seeing me get raped and beaten and everything, but it was just their imagination. None of those things happened. The shot was mostly just a close up on my face as we're talking. You don't see him do one thing to me. So that's something I'm really proud of as an actress.

JEWEL: Sounds like William Morris did well for you.

LISA: Actually, my mentor, Andy Keen, who owns one of the biggest film trailer companies, called Kaleidoscope Films, has always been one of my biggest supporters, and one of his best friends is Joe Heinz, who's head of publicity at Warner Brothers and one of Eastwood's best friends. Anyway, for years he kept telling me I wasn't ready for any big parts, until one day he said he found a part for me and that he'd set up a meeting. Well, I thought it was with a casting director, and I was coming from this McDonald's commercial where they had me with no make-up, hair in a fucking pony tail, freckles...looking like a geek. But the part was the young innocent girl, so I thought, "Great, perfect." But I get there and there's this bevy of beauties, all decked out in garter belts and fucking boas. I almost left. But I didn't, and I knock on this little bungalow and Clint

Eastwood opens the door...Now, there's very few people I truly admire in this business, but he's definitely one of them. Anyway, he tells me I've got the part as far as he's concerned but that I still have to read for the casting director, Marion Dougherty. Well, she's hard-core. She talks like this: *(gruff voice)* "All right, sweetheart, I'll be with you in a minute!" And I'm like, *(coy)* "Okay." So I read the whole scene and she said it was the best performance from a young actress she'd seen in five years.

JEWEL: Not to jump trains, but tell me about "Private Resort."

LISA: "Private Resort" was a pretty cool thing because I got to work with some incredible actors: Hector Elizondo, Tony Azito...it was also the first film of Andrew Dice Clay, and the second for Johnny Depp. We got to do a lot of ad-libbing, and it was fun...the story was just about these kids who take over this elegant resort. My character is on vacation with her boyfriend but he cheats on her, so I get bummed and decide to cheat on him. But the problem is we both wind up in the same suite.

JEWEL: Now, weren't you in "California Suite"?

LISA: Actually, just the trailer. See, I was working at the time for Andy at Kaleidoscope, delivering film, and I took this one can over to Ray Stark, who told me I had a great look. Well, he doesn't know it, I'm sure, but that kind of solidified my intent. Anyway, he and Andy decided to put me in the trailer for "California Suite" by shooting some extra footage. I wasn't in the movie, but that was the first time I'd ever seen myself up on the big screen...It was the same situation with Cheech and Chong's "Nice Dreams," where I played this demented ballerina, but only in the trailer.

JEWEL: Moving right along, what about "Savage Beach"?

Lisa with Clint Eastwood

LISA: I adore Andy and Arlene Sidaris. I was raised in a screaming family, and that's the way Andy is, but I feel like I'm right at home with my dad. The story is a James Bond spoof where the women are spies and the men are bimbos. But they get good reviews because the producers aren't trying to do anything except make a low budget, fun film. They give young actors a chance to learn and grow, plus they shoot in Hawaii and that's an added incentive.

JEWEL: I'd imagine you get fan mail from all this?

LISA: Oh yeah, and I get some real scary ones, too. When I was at CBS I got this letter from this total freak who would write stuff like "I saw you walking down the street and I don't want you wearing that green dress anymore." The weird thing is that Josie Cotton, who had this single out at the same time called "Johnny, Are You

Queer?" was getting the same letters as me, from the same guy. CBS almost called the FBI. Sometimes I even have nightmares about it. That stopped me from writing back to most of my fans, unless it's something really innocent.

JEWEL: So how does your family feel about seeing you in these kinds of movies?

LISA: Well, my dad wanted sons, so he raised my sisters and me to have this real aggressive, man's attitude, which I love. My little sister's name is even Larry. *(laughs)* But both my parents have said before, "With your brains, what are you doing being a dumb actor?" They're pleased, though, with what I've done.

JEWEL: Have you ever suffered through the "casting couch" nightmare?

LISA: I've been on so few interviews. Most of the things on my resumé were so...it seems like I've always managed to go right to the top, to Clint Eastwood, to Burt Reynolds. And these guys have such integrity. They never pull that kind of crap. It's just the little peons who do. Plus, all the low budget films I've done have been with very nice people.

JEWEL: But do the casting people ever look at your résumé and see "Savage Beach" and "Private Resort" and get this snide attitude?

LISA: Of course. But there's no such thing in my eyes as a small part. Even if it's the worst material, if you have charisma, it will shine through. I'm a firm believer in that. Also, it's how you present yourself. I don't come across as some bimbo. I won't dress differently for anyone. Fuck that shit. I'm proud of how I look.

JEWEL: So what's your opinion on doing nudity?

LISA: I have no problem at all if it's done tastefully and integrated into the plot. Of course, I'm going to be happier doing it in a big budget film where there are clear cut standards, but I really having nothing against nudity, even on low budget stuff. In fact, my only nightmare scenarios have involved theatrical agents, not producers.

JEWEL: How do you feel about depicting violence against women on screen?

LISA: Well, I did a rape scene in "Final Blow," which also starred Martin Landau. For that, I did some research at the UCLA Center for Rape Victims...and I think that, unfortunately, women are still second-rate citizens in our business. We're always treated a certain way...so any time I get a chance to portray any kind of reality, I feel like that's my responsibility as an actress. That includes nudity and violence, because that is part of reality for women. Obviously, though, if something is done in revoltingly bad taste then I wouldn't do it. But let's face it, the reality of the world is pretty grim.

JEWEL: Any skeletons in your closet?

LISA: There were a lot of times I needed money and rather than get a nine-to-five job...I was floundering in every emotional, spiritual way possible and I did some nude photographs. They were basically just topless, but I can't stand the fact that I let myself be manipulated by any schmuck.

JEWEL: Do you have any specific career goals for the next five years?

LISA: I'm producing now. Features and comedy shorts. I'm also involved in A.A. and we have this script that I developed for me to star in. It's called "Kick the Can." Right now, that's my life. I won't rest until it's done. And there's been some incredible interest. At first the producing thing was just to help me show what I could do as an actress, but now it's more than that. I've got a couple other projects, a studio's going to be doing one of them. I also want to do theatre.

JEWEL: Do you see yourself ever having a family?

LISA: Oh, God, here we go...One day I see myself having a kid. But I'm definitely not ready at all. No comment, though on matrimony. In fact, I have this saying that the only thing "matrimony" and "fidelity" have in common is that they both end in "y." I'm just such a schizoid, it's so hard for me to commit to one person.

JEWEL: Who do you most admire?

LISA: Vivien Leigh. I respect her work so much. And living today, Isabelle Adjani, who I've actually been compared to and that's a total ego stroke.

JEWEL: Any regrets through it all?

LISA: I know it seems like everything came so easily to me, but I really did work my ass off. I'm a workaholic. And now I have a tremendous sense of urgency, like maybe I wasted time, like I should've been doing what I'm doing now, producing, sooner.

JEWEL: You know what they say, "You're the sum of all your experiences."

LISA: All I want to do with my acting and producing is just be in a position to do quality work all the time.

JEWEL: If you could speak out against anything, what would it be?

LISA: I'm definitely becoming more involved in saving our planet. And I can't wait until the time when my voice will matter at all because I'm one of those people who, once I get committed to something, nothing will stop me from making a change. The other thing is child abuse. I really feel strongly about this...but right now I have to be selfish and commit to what I'm doing, so that I'll have a chance to make a difference.

"...on a bad day, I would get into the self-pity thing...and start wondering why I was asking people how they liked their steak."

Kelli Maroney

Interviewing all these actresses, I find myself learning a lot, being impressed with different things about different people. I was most impressed with Kelli Maroney's attitude, her ability to carry on despite setbacks that would have stopped someone of lesser spirit. Everyone in this business encounters ups and downs — sometimes very extreme ones — and how you deal with them obviously has a lot to do with whether you survive in acting or go elsewhere. Kelli started on a big-time soap and her career has been a roller coaster ever since. But, with the spirit she demonstrates, it's obvious that the "up" parts will always win out for her.

JEWEL: What's your background?

KELLI: I grew up in Minneapolis. My parents were Catholic. My mother was a bookkeeper. My father taught high school. All my brothers and sisters were 15-20 years older than me. I was what you might call a Catholic accident.

JEWEL: Did you buy into the whole Catholic experience?

KELLI: I think I was like every good Catholic girl. I went through that period before puberty where you want to be a nun. Then you get your period, a cute guy starts liking you and there goes being a nun.

JEWEL: Were your parents strict?

KELLI: My father was very strict. But he died when I was 14. My mother had me when she was 44. There were a lot of things she wanted to do in her life, things she had never done. So her attitude with me was, "Whatever you want to do, get out there and do it."

JEWEL: What was there to do for recreation in Minnesota?

KELLI: I watched a lot of movies. All the old movies on TV. And I read constantly. Everything from Nancy Drew to romance novels...

JEWEL: What were your fantasies?

KELLI: I wanted to be beautiful and wealthy. All the old movie stars seemed to have everything all together. Everyone loved them, they had everything they wanted.

JEWEL: When did you decide you wanted to be an actress?

KELLI: From the very beginning. But I was embarrassed to tell anyone. Especially my father. In the midwest if you tell people you want to be an actress, you get laughed out of the room.

JEWEL: So what was your plan of attack? How did you think you were going

71

to storm Hollywood?

KELLI: I had no idea. I mean, none of my schools ever had a drama department. Being an actress was just a fantasy, all in my head. Then, when I was seventeen, my mother found an ad in the paper. They were looking for people at the Guthrie Theatre to be apprentices. I pestered them and pestered them, until the manager finally conceded that anyone who called as much as me was going to be enthusiastic and responsible. It was a long way from being a star and the envy of everyone in Minnesota, but I soon decided I wanted to devote my life to classical theatre.

JEWEL: What did your mother say when she saw you up on stage that first time?

KELLI: She said, and to this day always reminds me, that if she hadn't seen that ad for the Guthrie Theatre, I'd probably be a housewife in Minnesota.

JEWEL: When did you make the move for Hollywood?

KELLI: Well, first I went east to enroll in a conservatory program: The National Shakespeare Company. But when I got off the plane in New York, I had no money. My plan was to work at Blimpie's and study.

JEWEL: Sounds like some plan.

KELLI: *(chuckling)* Yeah, but that's been the way with my whole career. I never really had much of a plan. Anyway, when I was looking for an apartment, this real estate broker told me she had a friend who was an agent, and they were looking for a sex kitten for "Ryan's Hope." Well, I thought for sure this was a secret porno ring, but I checked it out anyway.

JEWEL: That's right, you were on "Ryan's Hope."

KELLI: Less than two weeks in New York and I get this plum part on a soap. I was so nervous at the audition. I was shaking like a leaf. But this was my dream coming true. I made it happen. My desire was so strong, I think I willed those people to give me the part.

JEWEL: So there you were, on a soap. Did you have any experience in front of a camera?

KELLI: None. I was totally green. I'd never seen a TV camera. In fact, I had never even seen the show.

JEWEL: Did the show regulars accept you?

KELLI: Not at first. But then they saw how hard I was willing to work. Eventually they accepted me.

JEWEL: How long were you on the show?

KELLI: Three years.

JEWEL: You must have gone through some major emotional changes. Going from a small-town midwestern girl to a TV soap star...

KELLI: I was so focused on what I was doing, and the hours were so long, it took a while for the fame to hit me. Then one day I went in a deli for a sandwich and somebody said to me, "I know who you are." At first I didn't get it. I was terrified. I thought it was some psycho from Minneapolis. But he said I was Kimberly [from the show] and started talking about my character's storyline. In about ten seconds I went from being terrified to being on top of the world. That's when I knew what being a star was like.

JEWEL: What about New York? Was there any kind of culture shock for you?

KELLI: I think at that age it doesn't faze you as much. When you're older, there are things you would never do. But at that age, you just do what you want to do without really thinking about it.

JEWEL: So when did you come out to Hollywood?

KELLI: Well, after the first two years, they wrote off my character [on "Ryan's Hope"]. Then —

JEWEL: Wait, I thought you were on for three years.

KELLI: It's kind of complicated, but I'll come back to that. Anyway, thinking I was off the show, I auditioned for the lead in "Fast Times at Ridgemont High." I didn't get it, but they gave me the part of the Spirit Bunny, the cheerleader. So I came out here to California and did the role. I wanted to stay but, once again, I had no plan. No car, no plan. Nothing.

JEWEL: Was your experience on that movie different from "Ryan's Hope"?

KELLI: Oh, yeah. This was being a "movie" actress. Which was closer to my fantasy.

JEWEL: There were a lot of future stars in that movie: Sean Penn, Forest Whitaker, Judge Reinhold, Jennifer Jason Leigh and on and on. Did you get the sense back then that these people were destined for greatness?

KELLI: I had a sense that they were great then! Everybody on the set kind of stood out in my mind.

JEWEL: So how did that third year on the soap come about?

KELLI: They called me up and offered me a higher salary if I came back. But when that year ended, I knew I wanted to get back into movies. I'd had a taste of it and I wanted more. Plus, I had this fear that if I continued on TV, I would be stuck there and just known for that...so I came back out here.

JEWEL: What was the first audition you had?

KELLI: "Night of the Comet." But I didn't hear anything for a long time. So I went back to New York for a while — I still considered New York my home. While I was there, I auditioned for "The Purple Rose of Cairo." And I got the part, which was as Jeff Daniel's love interest in the film within the film...if that makes any sense.

JEWEL: If you've seen the movie, yeah.

KELLI: Anyway, that project died. Most people don't know it, but even Woody Allen has trouble getting his financing together. The project just got put on hold.

JEWEL: But you did get to meet Woody, didn't you?

KELLI: Yes. And he is the most charismatic, sexy man I've ever met.

JEWEL: *(shocked)* Sexy!?

KELLI: I know. I never thought of him like that from his movies, but in person he has so much personal power. You can't help but be in awe...

JEWEL: By the way, who's your acting idol?

KELLI: Well, the place where I get my dry cleaning done, the guy asked me for my picture to put up on the wall. I told him yes, but only if I could be next to Shirley MacLaine. *(laughs)*

JEWEL: Okay, so what happened with "Night of the Comet"?

KELLI: I finally got the part of Samantha. The story is, there's these two sisters and it's the end of the world — the world has been annihilated by a comet. And the only people who survive are those protected by steel. But some people are turning into zombies who have to drink blood to stay alive. It's kind of a sci-fi comedy, although when we were filming it we didn't know if it was going to be a comedy or not. The producers were actually considering filming two different versions.

JEWEL: That must have been a scary feeling, not knowing where to go with your character? Or what the tone was?

KELLI: It was very scary. But the worst part was, halfway through filming, I got a call from New York that Woody's movie was a "go" again. I begged the producers of "Night of the Comet" to rearrange my schedule so I could do the role...but it didn't work out.

JEWEL: How did you keep up your enthusiasm for "N.O.T.C"?

KELLI: Well, I just resolved that I was going to make that film the best it could be. Give one thousand percent.

JEWEL: Speaking of giving, has anyone ever asked you to...how shall I say, compromise your morals? *(pause)* Like taking off your clothes or...

KELLI: No. Thank God. I know lots of other girls have gotten that but, thankfully, I have never gotten into that position.

JEWEL: All right, after "N.O.T.C." what did you do?

KELLI: As you know, in L.A. you need a tape [of your acting]. But all I had was soap opera clips. So nobody knew who I was and no one was interested in seeing me for film work. Eventually I ran out of money and went back to New York. I did a small part on another soap opera, "One Life to Live," and just waited for "N.O.T.C." to come out. When it finally did, it got good reviews and I was so excited. But my timing was bad. By the time I got back out to L.A., people had already forgotten about the movie. I should've been there when the movie was hot, but I wasn't. Timing is everything...

JEWEL: Through all this moving, did you have a love life?

KELLI: One of the things I used to do was to isolate myself. I didn't think anyone could possibly understand what I was going through, so I just kept to myself. But I couldn't operate that way. Things started eating me up inside. *(pause)* Because I isolated myself so much, it seemed like I had no one to talk to. So I started drinking and became alcoholic. I got hepatitis and dropped out of the industry to recover. Since then, I've learned to divorce myself from my career. I've learned not to let my career consume me like it did before. It took about three years, but I've won a major fight, and now I've got the support system I need.

JEWEL: After you recovered, what was your attitude?

KELLI: My attitude was the same, I still loved acting. But people's attitude in the industry was like, "Where have you been these last few years?" I wanted to be straight-forward, but at the same time, you don't need to tell your life story.

JEWEL: So you're back in the loop? What's current?

KELLI: I read for "Cheers." I just did "Servants of Twilight" for Showtime and some other things. It's all about meeting people again...

JEWEL: During your recovery, how did you support yourself?

KELLI: Oh, waiting tables and stuff.

JEWEL: Did people ever recognize you?

KELLI: On a good day, I would realize how lucky I am that people remember me and like me and seem to care how I am. But on a bad day, I would get into the self-pity thing...and start wondering why I was asking people how they liked their steak.

JEWEL: But you stuck with it and you're back on track.

KELLI: Yeah, I've got a boyfriend and a good manager. I'm finally realizing that life is not about what parts you get. It's more about the other people in your life...what you can do for them, what you have to offer.

Photo by Dan Golden

JEWEL: In a larger way, is there anything you want to offer to the world as a whole, aside from entertainment?

KELLI: I think everyone should take care of their own corner of the garden. That means however they deal with other people, they should use passion and integrity. Not, "What can I get?" but, "What can I give?" I try for an attitude of total harmlessness.

JEWEL: Have you ever thought about getting back into the theatre?

KELLI: Yeah. I'm still involved in the Renegade Theatre Company. I want to get back to basics. I mean, last week we painted and dry-walled the sets. *(laughs)* It was actually fun.

"You are not a victim unless you choose to be. So anyone who considers being a stripper or a whatever to be degrading is wrong."

Karen Mayo Chandler

Playboy billed her as Jack Nicholson's ex-girl friend when she posed nude for their pages. It was true and it was a tremendous attention-getter: Beauty *and* an interesting story. Karen Mayo Chandler is a good example of someone who has been able to take control of her career, even when at her lowest points, and bring it back with a flourish. I was impressed with her determination and positive thinking. You doubtlessly will be, as well...

JEWEL: Okay, let's start from the beginning...

KAREN: I was born in Sutton Sory, England. My father was an electrical contractor, but he always wanted to be an actor. My mother worked in accounting. She had an artistic side to her, too. She was a glass engraver. In fact, she used to engrave goblets for the royal family and stuff like that.

JEWEL: Now, did your father encourage or discourage you from acting?

KAREN: Well, his parents wouldn't let him go into acting, but I sort of rebelled. I wanted to be an actress for as long as I can remember. I wanted to be a child star and I drove my parents so crazy, they finally let me go to stage school. I just sat on the stairs and screamed until they gave in. I was ten at the time.

JEWEL: But you were still going to regular school, too?

KAREN: Right. I had to work twice as hard. I ended up going to three different performance schools. The first one, my parents didn't think was academically good enough. The second one was too strict. We had to wear uniforms and curtsy to the headmaster. I mean, can you imagine me doing this? That was not my style. I was actually expelled from that one. Then I went to a place that was kind of a compromise between the two.

JEWEL: Why were you expelled?

KAREN: I was pretty crazy. I wore an antique wedding dress to a school party and got drunk. I was about thirteen at the time. I used to go out all the time to nightclubs, telling my parents I was spending the night with friends. I mean, I was having sex at age thirteen. I was terrible. I can remember doing drugs and falling asleep in class. The wedding dress was just the last straw, I suppose.

JEWEL: Were you popular in school?

KAREN: Very popular. I was the bad girl who had the courage to do all the things everybody else wanted to do.

JEWEL: What happened after school?

KAREN: I started a modeling career. I did work for *Harper's* and *Vogue*. By the time I was eighteen, I'd done at least fifty covers. And by the time I was twenty, I'd done about a hundred.

JEWEL: So suddenly you were living in the fast lane...

KAREN: Actually, after being such a rebellious girl, I kind of went the other way and played it straight. I remember going to Milan, my first time away from home, and there were all these lecherous old men. Our agent was practically procuring the models. There was this one guy who said he wanted me for the cover of *Harper's*, but that it meant going to Fiji and being his girlfriend. I mean, I was, like, sixteen! Needless to say, I wasn't very successful in Milan.

JEWEL: Did your parents support you on this?

KAREN: Yes, they were very proud of me. But they didn't know about the seedy side. Actually, it wasn't that seedy, not like Hollywood.

JEWEL: How long did you model?

KAREN: Until I was around twenty. Then I went back to acting school and I did this pantomime [an old English acting tradition] and that got me my union card, which is very hard to get. After that, I did quite a lot of television. I played a lot of princesses — sweet, naive princesses in series like "Flesh and Blood" and "Strangers." Why on Earth they cast me as a princess, I don't know. *(laughs)*

JEWEL: So what brought you to Hollywood?

KAREN: I had a relationship that wasn't working out. I just got sick of it and hopped on a plane with $1,000 in my pocket. I only knew one person. See, before I came out here, I'd just been on vacation with my mom, so I kind of knew the place. The second week I was here I got a job, a guest star role on the TV show "Bring 'Em Back Alive."

JEWEL: That didn't take long!

KAREN: Yeah, it was fast. But there was this model I knew who had an agent out here named David Wilder, and she took me in to meet with him. So I got chatting with him. He liked me and started sending me out. The third thing he sent me out on, I got, which got me my union papers over here.

JEWEL: You must've thought acting over here was a piece of cake.

KAREN: I thought everything would start happening immediately. But, of course, it didn't. I went back to England but then they flew me back because I was up for this part in "Blame It on Rio." I didn't get it, but I figured it was my destiny to stay in Hollywood. That first year was hell...

JEWEL: Did you have to succumb to getting a real job?

KAREN: Yeah, I was a babysitter in the evenings. And I was so broke, I was stealing toilet rolls and hot dogs from the refrigerator because I couldn't afford them. God, I know those mothers are going to kill me! *(laughs)* Also, my skin was breaking out from the heat, so the doctor put me on steroids, which blew me up so big, I couldn't model or act. All I could do was baby-sit.

JEWEL: Sounds like you hit a real low point.

KAREN: Yes, I was despondent, fat and pimply.

JEWEL: How did you pull yourself back up?

KAREN: I got off the steroids and started losing weight. I was also working out and had managed to get back into acting classes. I met a new agent at a dinner party and he got me a small part in "Beverly Hills Cop" as a receptionist. That was the turning point for me.

From "976-EVIL II" (1991), Courtesy Cinetel

JEWEL: How was it working with Eddie Murphy on an A-movie?

KAREN: Well, he wasn't such a mega-star then. He'd only done a couple movies and I think that he became really big after that film. I was only getting scale plus a little bit, so it didn't seem like such a big deal at the time, but I was kind of nervous. I didn't realize it would lead to other things, but it did. After that, I immediately got a movie, which I went to India to shoot, called "Chasing the Sword." It was a total nightmare that never got finished, so we won't talk about that one...

JEWEL: How did you deal with that picture falling through?

KAREN: I thought it was my big break, but I came back devastated. I didn't even get paid. When I got back, though, I got some little bitsy things. Then I got the part of Gwen Dudley on "The Young and the Restless." I played this conniving English bitch for about six or seven months until we ran into contract problems.

JEWEL: So did that success balance out the previous failure for you?

KAREN: My whole career has been like being on a yo-yo. I go from having terrible stuff happening to having wonderful stuff happen.

JEWEL: At this time, were you getting recognized as a nasty woman because of the part you played?

KAREN: People that came up to me were always really complimentary...there's something about bad characters that people like. Maybe it's because they have the courage to say and do things that others wouldn't. I did get some nasty fan mail, but it was more directed towards the character...letters telling Gwen, "Hands off so-and-so...he's my favorite character!"

JEWEL: Does it bother you that people take these things so seriously?

KAREN: Actually I never had any real incidents on the show, but after the *Playboy* article, I started having incidents. For instance, I received a box of shit in the mail. My car was also broken into and vandalized four times. But there was nothing I could do, because no one saw who was doing any of this.

JEWEL: You're talking about the infamous *Playboy* article where you discuss your, uh, relationship with Jack Nicholson, right?

KAREN: *(laughs)* I'm never going to live this down, am I?

JEWEL: I'd imagine it was hard to make your relationship public.

KAREN: Actually I was sick to death being plagued by it...Jack has his standard "No comment!," but I was being hounded by the press and I got sick of it. After the relationship ended, I asked Jack what I should do and he said, "Do whatever you want. The press is just as good for me as it is for you." So I did.

JEWEL: How did you meet Jack?

KAREN: I met him in Aspen. We were both up there skiing. I was on vacation with a girlfriend and we got invited to a dinner party at Jack's house, but I didn't get involved with him until a long while after that...I knew he was trouble from the word "Go."

JEWEL: So what's the truth about the bondage and all that?

KAREN: *(laughs)* I'm a little outspoken, what can I say? *(pause)* I mean, I was sick of all the questions...I'm a little bit rebellious.

JEWEL: But did he really tie you up?

KAREN: *(laughs)* Handcuffs, my dear. Handcuffs...and it was wonderful. Now Jack has a new image!

JEWEL: What did he think about the article?

KAREN: A girl's got to do what a girl's got to do. I mean, Jack didn't think I would take it as far as I did. But he also knows what I'm all about, that I've never been one to be intimidated by the press. I've always been outspoken, even if it upsets people. I prefer honesty. I prefer that approach.

JEWEL: Has that article had any effect on your potential boyfriends since then?

KAREN: Some people sit in judgment over it, but no one has the right to. Other people are intrigued by it...the most interesting comment I heard was from a casting director who said, "Well, Karen, it seems you've had quite a lot of notoriety since I last saw you. Have you had any time to do any acting?" *(laughs)* To me, that was just perfect! But you know, since then men go out with me and expect me to attack them at the end of the evening. And they're very disappointed.

JEWEL: How did you feel about doing the nude layout along with the article?

KAREN: Actually, it was my idea to talk about Jack. They were doing a celebrity pictorial on up-and-coming actresses and I just got a little more explicit with my relationship than they expected. They just kind of ran with it.

JEWEL: Now, didn't you do a few movies during that year you spent with Jack?

KAREN: Yeah, five. There was one epic in Mexico, a little B-movie called "The Island Love"...although they might've changed the title. It was a typical B-movie. I played this top model who's been divorced from her husband, the guy who made her what she was. Anyway, we end up, through supernatural causes, working together on this island where they spent their honeymoon. I know the movie's been sold to *Playboy*.

JEWEL: So it probably has a lot of nudity in it...

KAREN: This idea of exploitation...I don't know. Some of the scripts have been good, others haven't. I think some people think that low budget movies have to have a certain amount of T-and-A in them. But some of the movies I've done have been more like art films. Although you wouldn't think it, I'm actually very straight — from my strict British upbringing. So doing these movies lets me go kind of crazy. And to be perfectly honest, sometimes I enjoy taking my clothes off! *(laughs)*

JEWEL: What were some of the other films you did?

KAREN: "Out of the Dark," with Tab Hunter, Karen Black and Divine. It was an arty film. I played this girl who worked for a phone sex company. All the girls get killed by the person you least suspect. I also did a small part in "Take Two." Then there was "Stripped to Kill."

JEWEL: How do you like playing phone sex operators and strippers?

KAREN: I enjoy playing those parts. I really do. I don't know why.

JEWEL: But don't you worry about these roles being degrading towards women?

KAREN: No, I really don't. I think that people do things out of choice. You are not a victim unless you choose to be. So anyone who considers being a stripper or a whatever to be degrading is wrong. If a woman can work a situation to her advantage, I don't sit in judgment over her. If a woman ends up with a man who beats her, she has chosen not to leave for whatever her reasons. I don't believe what I'm doing is anything more than depicting an element of true life — just like those men I dated were disappointed I didn't attack them, most people are disappointed to learn I'm not like the characters I portray. I'm not the bitch I was on "Young and the Restless." Yes, there is an element of me, but...

JEWEL: What about "Savage Harbor"?

KAREN: I think they might have changed that to "Death Feud," I'm not sure. I played a junkie hooker in that one. I did quite a bit of research on that one actually. I even went so far as to get drops to dilate my pupils.

JEWEL: And "African Express"?

KAREN: That was a slight change of direction...No sex! No nudity! Not even a kiss! I played an American tomboy pilot in 1942. It was a total change of character for me. I was very pleased about it.

JEWEL: Do you have big expectations for yourself over the next few years?

KAREN: I want to do better-crafted projects. But in terms of characters, I don't want to set any limitations for myself. I want to play characters with some sort of an edge to them, but not necessarily always bad girls. I wouldn't mind playing a good girl, someone you could admire.

JEWEL: Who do you admire most?

KAREN: Anne Boleyn.

JEWEL: Are we talking about the same Anne Boleyn who was King Henry the Eighth's wife? The one that was beheaded?

KAREN: She changed the religion of the country. She achieved the impossible. She was the second wife of Henry VIII and the country was very Catholic. She got herself pregnant and held out, determined not just to be his mistress. I read about her as a kid and I always admired her courage.

JEWEL: Are there any causes you support, either financially or otherwise?

KAREN: I give money to help abused children. I believe that you have to give back something. Whatever success you achieve, you have to give back some way. There are two things that really got my attention when I started considering how I could give back: The elderly and how they are dismissed, and the children because they are the next generation. I just feel that the abuse to them is what creates so many of the problems we have.

JEWEL: While we're on the subject of abuse...Have you ever been subjected to a "casting couch" nightmare?

KAREN: Yes, I have. The one thing that comes to mind...actually it happened twice. When I first came to town, I was still a little naive on how things were run. There were two legitimate producers who had me read, but they were the ones who read with me. And they picked the classic love story. So while the scene unfolded they started rubbing their hands all over and trying to kiss me...you're in shock! You don't know whether to say, "Get your dirty hands off me!" or just be professional about it and act along. But then you don't know how far to let them take it. That kind of thing's happened to me twice and, needless to say, I got up and left and didn't get the job — if there was even a job to get! (laughs)

JEWEL: What was the other instance?

KAREN: There was this interview for...this guy was a real bastard. It was a bad girl role where she was supposed to seduce this guy. Well, the director is videotaping the audition and the producer is playing this other guy. The director says, "Really go for it," so I start unbuttoning this producer's shirt and really flirting with him and he looks kind of embarrassed. Then afterward, he wanted to go to lunch and "discuss things." Well, I just told him I didn't mix business with pleasure and left. As fate would have it, about two months later I had another agent who sent me out on this audition for a totally different role but in the same project, which still hadn't gotten off the ground. So we just did a chit-chat interview, but this time he's got this wonderful attitude with me since I totally rejected him. Afterwards, he calls my agent and says, "Don't represent that girl. She's very unprofessional. She tried to rape me during the course of the interview." And I said, "He should be so lucky!"

JEWEL: You've been killed in a lot of your movies. When you see yourself get killed, does it create any kind of strange sensation for you?

KAREN: The only time that happened was with "Out of the Dark," and just because it seemed so realistic. It was scary.

JEWEL: How were you killed in that one?

KAREN: By a clown with a garden hose...but it was the circumstances. It was raining that night and I was in this skimpy outfit. It was late and I thought I was going to die just from exhaustion and from the freezing cold. So when I see the movie I recall the whole experience, not just the garden hose.

JEWEL: You mentioned earlier that conveying sex or nudity on screen doesn't bother you, but what about violence? What about how this affects children?

KAREN: The only thing that would worry me is exploiting very young children in a sexual manner. That upsets me.

JEWEL: Lastly, is there anything you would change about your life if you could?

KAREN: I think, in retrospect, I should have gone to New York and modeled while I could...maybe gone that route and done theatre instead. But that's the only regret I really have.

From "African Express" (1989)

"People may see me as a sexual vamp-type, but that is not me at all. I'm a country girl at heart."

Caroline Munro

L ike Martine Beswicke, elsewhere in this book, Caroline Munro has earned the badge of being a "Bond Girl" and has racked up a truly impressive list of appearances in horror movies and science-fiction films. The latter have included portraying Vincent Price's spouse in two "Dr. Phibes" films and being bitten by Christopher Lee in "Dracula Today." When I spoke with her, I was impressed with how polite she was and how she approached acting with a very light-hearted attitude while still managing to be serious about her work.

JEWEL: You know, I used to live in England, on Great Portland Street near Devonshire.

CAROLINE: Well, I was born across from Windsor Castle in a nursing home and lived for the first few years in Richmond, which is about twelve miles out of London. Then we moved down to the sea, to Brighton, which was beautiful. I went to a convent down there.

JEWEL: *(confused)* A convent?

CAROLINE: *(laughs)* It's a private school run by nuns. Lots of girls attend them. I wasn't a boarder, though. I went home every night.

JEWEL: What do your parents do?

CAROLINE: My mother helps out with charities. She's done that for many years. My father is a solicitor...oh, but that also has a different connotation over there, doesn't it? Solicitor, as in lawyer.

JEWEL: Are you still close with your family?

CAROLINE: Actually, I just walked in the door five minutes ago from seeing them. They still live in Richmond, which is only twelve miles away. I see them two or three times a week. We're very close.

JEWEL: So did you enjoy this convent school?

CAROLINE: Oh, it was lovely, mostly girls. There were boys, but just little boys up to age eight.

JEWEL: Do you feel like you missed out on establishing boyfriend-girlfriend relationships?

CAROLINE: I suppose I did. I came out when I was sixteen-and-a-half and I did feel pretty sheltered. It was kind of a shock when I first met boys *(laughs)*.

JEWEL: So you never really got a chance to experience puppy love?

CAROLINE: *(laughs)* I had mine with the Beatles! *(laughs)* Puppy love was Paul McCartney. And before that it was Davy Crockett. My mother even bought me a Davy Crockett hat and a little gun. I used to march around the house. My dad took me to see the film six times. He was my hero.

JEWEL: When did you finally have your first boyfriend?

CAROLINE: I got quite a late start actually because I started work right after school and didn't have much time for boys. But I suppose my first boyfriend came when I was 18. It was nice, it was lovely.

JEWEL: So you graduated at around 16, then you started to work. That sounds different from how it works in the States...

CAROLINE: It's totally different. You don't have graduation actually...if you want to go to a university you take exams, and, depending on what your grades you get, you either go to a university or a college. But I didn't. I wanted to do art; I was mad keen on interior design.

JEWEL: So when did you make the transition into modeling and acting?

CAROLINE: There was an art student friend of mine who was studying photography and he asked if he could take some pictures of me. I said, "Oh, yes, lovely." And the pictures turned out nice, so he sent them to a newspaper competition.

JEWEL: Was this newspaper *The Sun?*

CAROLINE: Oh no, nothing like that! *(laughs)* This was way, way, way back, like, in 1968, and there weren't any topless pictures or anything like that then. This was all very straight-laced...

JEWEL: So what was the response to the pictures?

CAROLINE: Well, a very well known photographer was the judge of the competition. His name was David Bailey. He was married to Jean Shrimpton, who must have been the greatest model of all time, before Twiggy...anyway, the photographs won. After that I started modeling pretty quickly.

JEWEL: You were the Lands Navy Rum Girl, weren't you?

CAROLINE: Yes, I was. *(laughs)* For 12 years and I didn't even have a contract. They just used to phone me up and say, "Do you want to do another one?" So we'd do another one.

JEWEL: How was the money back then?

CAROLINE: English wages don't compare to the States. It's much more money in the States.

JEWEL: Did you ever have to do anything strange when you were going out on interviews?

CAROLINE: Oh gosh, it was so long ago...but I remember I went up for this Dr. Pepper commercial, which was fairly recent actually, and I was like this creature, this barmaid with three legs.

JEWEL: I saw that...where the aliens come down and —

CAROLINE: That's it! I had a very strange hairdo, *(laughs)* things standing on end...This chap comes in and he's asking for a Dr. Pepper and I keep giving him these very strange drinks with eyeballs and exploding things in them, and there are all these aliens around. Anyway, he thinks that I'm pretty normal after I give him the Dr. Pepper, but then I come around the bar and sit beside him and cross my legs, all three of them! *(laughs)*

JEWEL: So how did you get into films?

CAROLINE: Apparently, the man who used to be the head of Hammer Films traveled up and down on the train to Brighton and he kept seeing my Land's Navy Rum billboard. Eventually, he said to his sidekick, "See if you can find that girl." Well, they tracked me down and I went to see them. We got on really well and they signed me to a year's contract.

JEWEL: This sounds like the old days with the studios where you sign a contract and do any film they want?

CAROLINE: Exactly. If you're right for the part.

JEWEL: What was your first film?

CAROLINE: "Dracula A.D. '72" with Peter Cushing and Christopher Lee. I got killed off in the first reel.

JEWEL: Were you disappointed with that?

CAROLINE: I didn't feel too bad. I thought, "At least I've gotten started and maybe next time I'll survive a little longer! *(laughs)* Also, I thoroughly enjoyed the experience of working with wonderful people. In fact, I was with Peter Cushing last week. He was on a show over here called "This is Your Life."

JEWEL: Were you one of the guests?

CAROLINE: Yes, I was. It was lovely to see him again. He's such a dear man. Gentle, funny and clever...He was really overcome with seeing everyone like Peter Ustinov, Ursula Andress, Sir John Mills. It was a really good show.

JEWEL: Did you tell anyone that you were in "Dracula A.D. '72?"

CAROLINE: I didn't tell anyone, really. It's just another job, really, isn't it?

JEWEL: But didn't people recognize you?

CAROLINE: They did...and if I thought the work was OK, I'd say, "Well, thanks very much." Or if it wasn't, I'd say, "Well, it's not one of my better things." It's strange, really. It's your other self doing the work. It's like any other job. You just do it to the best of your ability, and if people like it, that's wonderful. But truthfully, there've been very few times in my career that I've been happy with my performances. They're getting better, the older I get, but it's taken me a long time, since I didn't have any formal acting training.

JEWEL: Did that make you feel insecure?

CAROLINE: Yes, because you don't have that technique to fall back on. But

I've come to the conclusion that if you want to do stage work, training is essential. Film is different, though, because it's much smaller and more intimate. Even though you're blown way up on screen, it's all got to do with feeling, not technique. Look at Marilyn Monroe, she was trained later on, but she started out as a model. She had a wonderful way with the camera, very natural and uninhibited.

JEWEL: Did you ever have a mentor, someone who helped your career along?

CAROLINE: No, but my parents were always there. The key for me was never to take it too seriously. When they say, "It's a wrap," you have to go home and cook your supper and just switch off. You've got to have another life, or otherwise you go insane.

JEWEL: Are you married?

CAROLINE: Actually, I am. I just got married last Monday! *(laughs)*

JEWEL: That's great! *(laughs)* Is this your first time?

CAROLINE: No, it's my second time and my last time.

JEWEL: What does your husband do?

CAROLINE: He's in the film business too. He created "Max Headroom." His name is George Dugdale. His production company, Coast to Coast Production, is doing a movie right now called "Dr. Who."

JEWEL: Are you going to be in that?

CAROLINE: I think I'm going to play a baddie.

JEWEL: Now, I understand you've never had a manager. Was it tough always pushing for yourself?

CAROLINE: It felt good, actually, because whatever I got, I got on my own merits...but I'm in a bad situation at the moment. I just finished a film in Italy. "Out of the Depths" was the working title but I think it's called "The Black Cat" now. It's a great little film and good script, but they haven't paid me yet.

JEWEL: That's where an agent would come in handy.

CAROLINE: Actually, I do have an agent at ICM. But when I signed to do the film, my agent was very ill, so no one was really dealing with this situation.

JEWEL: Do you get a lot of fan mail from the States?

CAROLINE: Yes. They send it to ICM and ICM sends it along to me. I'm a bit naughty about replying. I get on binges where I do reply, but it's a big undertaking because they all want photographs and it's a very expensive proposition. I've got a chap in the United States who runs a fan club over there, so at least he takes care of that end for me.

JEWEL: Have you ever received any scary letters?

CAROLINE: There's one chap from the States who kept writing that he was my long lost cousin in prison. But nothing nasty. I've been very lucky. I suppose it depends on the type of films you do. If you attract controversy, then that sets the funny ones going. Most of my fans like "Sinbad" the best.

JEWEL: Do you have a favorite film you've done?

CAROLINE: I've enjoyed certain elements in everyone of them. One of my favorites, though, was a film called "Captain Kronos, Vampire Hunter" way back in '71 or '72. I played a gypsy girl, who was closer to me than most of my roles.

JEWEL: Do you think that you have developed a "bad girl" image because you've played so many evil women?

CAROLINE: I suppose so. People may see me as a sexual vamp-type, but that is not me at all. I'm a country girl at heart. I climb mountains and have a little doggie...but if they want me to play the villain, I can play it.

With Joe Spinell on the set of "The Last Horror Film" (1984)

JEWEL: Have you ever considered moving to the States?

CAROLINE: I'd love to work more over there. In fact, I went to New York two years ago and had the possibility of working on a soap opera there, "The Guiding Light," I think it was...but you have to sign a five year contract and I have my family here. Whether I made the right choice or not, I don't know. I'm very much a homebody and acting is not my total life. It's a wonderful part of it and I've had a terrific experience, but I'm not ambitious to be a huge star.

JEWEL: Is there any director you'd like to work for?

CAROLINE: Oh, anything with Spielberg! Something modern day, something to sink your teeth into. I always seem to be the baddie, I don't know. Maybe they always think of dark-haired women as bad. I think it can be the reverse...It would just be nice to play something more realistic. With terrific actors, obviously.

JEWEL: Such as?

CAROLINE: I'd love to work with Robert DeNiro. I like him. And I like Bette Midler and Debra Winger. One of the funniest men I've ever worked with was Roger Moore. He's such a nice man. I did "The Spy Who Loved Me" with him. He has this habit of, just before the take starts, he'll suddenly throw in a one liner that'll throw you off. But it's relaxing.

JEWEL: Who do you most admire in the world?

CAROLINE: I'm pretty much in awe of my parents...and there was this very good poet, his name was John Birchman. He was very fascinating. And last night, I just watched a program on Winston Churchill. I didn't know him because it was before my time, but he was so fascinating. There's one man I'd like to have met!

JEWEL: Have your parents seen all your films?

CAROLINE: Oh no, not at all. *(laughs)* If they come on the telly, we see them. But a lot of my stuff, even I haven't seen. I just never get around to it. You're never entirely happy with it, I don't think. You always think it's going to be different.

JEWEL: Have you ever done any nudity in your films?

CAROLINE: No, I haven't, actually. The closest I got was the latest, this Italian one. But I don't really think it's necessary. It can be just as sexy or sensual with your clothes on. I think it's all in the imagination.

JEWEL: Have you been in any violent films?

CAROLINE: Yes, but I'm not overly keen on violence. If it's fantasy or something that we know is impossible, like Dracula, then I tend not to mind. But there was a film I did in the States called "Maniac" that I think was banned in Los Angeles. And I could see why when I saw the end result. Whether it promotes violence or not, I don't know. I think most young people know enough about special effects to realize that this isn't reality.

JEWEL: So what's your gameplan for say, the next ten years?

CAROLINE: After "Dr. Who," I don't know. I'm just terribly happy at the moment and it's very hard to imagine...I'm just looking forward to spending time with my husband.

"...they wanted me to dance topless with a midget...but I just felt it was too circusy."

Kitten Natividad

Francesca "Kitten" Natividad first came to the attention of film fans with her role as the Greek Chorus in skin-flick director supreme Russ Meyer's "Up!" The film's plot, co-devised with Meyer by noted film critic Roger Ebert, was so complicated as to require plot summations every five or ten minutes. That was where Kitten came in, popping up every now and then with the scorecard, explaining who was sleeping with whom and to what purpose. Like most women in a Russ Meyer film, she was nude and displaying a fantasy bustline. She instantly became a favorite of both Russ Meyer fans and Russ Meyer. Kitten appeared in dual (starring) roles in his next film, "Beneath the Valley of the Ultra-Vixens," and has since maintained a busy career on the stripping circuit and with frequent lead and guest star roles in such films as "My Tutor," "Taking It Off," "Taking It All Off" (the sequel), and others, usually playing a stripper or hooker.

JEWEL: What is your real name?

KITTEN: Francesca Isabel Natividad...I was born in Wattichiquaqua, Mexico. That's the border town of El Paso, Texas, which is where I really grew up. Living in El Paso's like living in Mexico. You still eat your tortillas and beans and speak fluent Spanish. It was a great life...but as soon as I became eighteen, I wanted to live in a big city.

JEWEL: Was it a poor environment you grew up in?

KITTEN: I never thought of us as poor, because we always had food to eat and I was always the little darling of my two grandmothers, so I was spoiled, with lots of clothes and stuff. I think we were middle class.

JEWEL: What did your parents do?

KITTEN: My mother divorced my father when I was about two or three, then remarried a real nice man. At first, she went to work in a blue jeans factory. He worked as a metallurgist, a doctor of metals.

JEWEL: How did your family come to America?

KITTEN: When my mother remarried, she remarried an American citizen who was also Mexican. Because of that she was made a citizen, too. And because we were under the age of 18, her children were automatic citizens. So we were very legal.

JEWEL: How many brothers and sisters do you have?

KITTEN: Well, it was a split family. I have five from one and four from the other. I'm closer to the ones on my mother's side because those are the ones I was raised with...but the other ones sometimes call me up and ask for autographs and stuff. They're here in California now.

JEWEL: What was your high school experience like?

KITTEN: Well, I used to be punk before punk was in. I used to dye my hair orange and my nickname was "Carrots." I also used to be very politically inclined, like, I was president of my senior class and director of the senior Steering Committee. I used to like to run things...and I could, because I never dated anyone from my school. I would flirt real bad and tease all these guys, but never give it up. I just wanted their vote.

JEWEL: Why were you rebellious? I mean, orange hair in El Paso must have raised a few eyebrows.

KITTEN: I wanted to stick out like a sore thumb.

JEWEL: Well, you probably did! *(laughs)* And what did your parents think of this?

KITTEN: I was always a good girl, made good grades. My mother let me do anything I wanted. Except go out

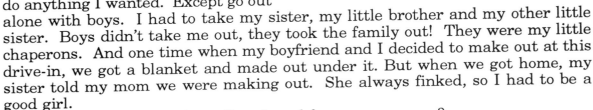

alone with boys. I had to take my sister, my little brother and my other little sister. Boys didn't take me out, they took the family out! They were my little chaperons. And one time when my boyfriend and I decided to make out at this drive-in, we got a blanket and made out under it. But when we got home, my sister told my mom we were making out. She always finked, so I had to be a good girl.

JEWEL: Were you, uh, well-endowed from a young age?

KITTEN: No, not until I was eighteen. I used to be very skinny. I had nice breasts, but because I always wore my boyfriend's letter jacket, no one could ever see them. I was a virgin until my graduation day, when I eloped with him. I had to save it for my husband. That's what everybody always told me in church. I was a very good little Catholic girl. But then the marriage was annulled because we were too young and it was done in Mexico.

JEWEL: Did you have aspirations of stardom back then?

KITTEN: I wanted to be a nurse for the longest time, but my mother said she couldn't put me through college. So I came to California and went to data processing school...then I started having so much fun here on the beach that I decided to take a year off school. Well, one of my girlfriend's sister was a go-go dancer and she'd come home with this big pile of tips. I said, "Gee, I want to do that!" So this girl took me to this agent who made me do a little dance for him.

JEWEL: There was an agent for go-go dancers?

KITTEN: Yes, because when you did go-go dancing, and this was twenty-two years ago, they would send you off to San Bernardino for two hour shifts. That's where it started. There were so many clubs, and you got paid $17 an hour, plus $100 in tips for every two-hour shift. I was making the bucks! And because I lived so far away, in Rosemead, I would work two hour shifts at several clubs before coming home. I was really skinny then from so much dancing.

JEWEL: That's all you did, was dance? You didn't have to take anything off?

KITTEN: You didn't have that much on to begin with. They would just put on music — I didn't get to pick it — and you'd dance on this stage. You'd just get up there and boogie.

JEWEL: What did your parents think of this?

KITTEN: They didn't talk to me for about two years, but it was what I wanted to do, so I didn't care. I was real stubborn. We got over it.

JEWEL: So you were doing the whole go-go circuit and making a bunch of money...

KITTEN: Yeah. Then I won the Miss Nude Universe, which was held at the Oakdale Nudist Camp. It's just like a beauty contest. And from then on, things just clicked. After I won the contest, I became a stripper, which meant you've actually got to put on a show...that's the difference between go-go dancing and stripping.

JEWEL: I remember you had a bathtub routine...

KITTEN: Yeah. I had this big fish bowl prop, and I'd get in there and do splish-splash. It wasn't anything new. It had been around for a long time, but I just put my own personality in it. Lili St. Cyr did it first. I did it for this club called The Losers on La Cienega [in Los Angeles] where they let me make it fun, instead of sultry...because I have a very bubbly personality. I feel ridiculous being sexy. I already am! Why have to try and be so dramatic? (laughs)

JEWEL: The Losers was a happening club, wasn't it?

KITTEN: Definitely...and after that, I toured around to different clubs. I

That's Kitten on the right.

even followed Blaze Starr, although I didn't work with her. I saw her show. She was probably in her forties then, getting a little fat. But she still had a bunch of little stage door Johnnies.

JEWEL: (amused) Stage door Johnnies!?

KITTEN: You know what groupies are, right? Well, these guys are old men who stand around the stage door and bring you chocolates and flowers. And a lot of them were johns...

JEWEL: What club did Russ Meyer discover you at?

KITTEN: He discovered me at the Classic Cat. It was right after Shari Eubanks did her show...she was the star of "Supervixens."

JEWEL: Where was the Classic Cat located?"

KITTEN: It was on Sunset, right across from Tower Records,

where Tower Video is now. It was the greatest club. It was so big. We all wore falsies and little bows down here.

JEWEL: Okay, so Russ came to see you at this club...

KITTEN: Shari had told him about me, so he came to see my show. He used me for this movie called "Up!," where I played the Greek Chorus, the narrator. After that, he liked my work and asked me to be in "Beneath...," just to play Lola LaGusta, but he couldn't find another person to play La Bonia, so overnight he rewrote the script and let me play both roles. That's when we started to fall in love. I even left my husband because Russ made me all these promises...I've done three films for him: "Up!," "Beneath the Valley of the Ultravixens" and "The Breast of Russ Meyer," which is not out yet. He put it aside to write his autobiography.

JEWEL: So you never got married?

KITTEN: We lived together for four years and he opened a lot of doors for me. I was still pretty young and everything was great, except that I still liked to go discoing and go to the beach, party with the girls...but Russ was older and he'd get so mad if I had girls over giggling and stuff. (*laughs*) Russ was a great help, though. I will never forget him and I learned a lot from him. For me, it will always be Kitten and Russ.

JEWEL: So while you were doing these films with Russ, did you continue stripping?

KITTEN: Yeah. Russ found that very much of a turn-on. And he's a workaholic, so I wanted to work a few days a week...I get a lot of my parts still from working at The Body Shop. Casting people come in and see me. That's how I got my parts in "Wild Life" and "My Tutor."

JEWEL: What did you do in "Wild Life"?

KITTEN: I played a stripper. I was also in "Airplane 2" and "Night Patrol." I can't remember the rest...I've done so many films, I don't care anymore. Wait, there was another one, "The Big House."

JEWEL: What was that about?

KITTEN: I played a stripper that's in jail. It's a funny movie...they tie me up and pin pasties on me. I don't remember, exactly. In almost every movie I played a stripper, a go-go dancer or a whore. But I won't do "X" movies.

JEWEL: What about "Titillation"? That was "X"?

KITTEN: I just played the girl who they're trying to catch. There's this eccentric, rich old man who makes a big bronze bra and says to all these people that anybody who can find someone to fit into this bra would get $50,000! So everyone was looking for me, but I never was in the sex scenes, which was good.

JEWEL: Did it bother you being associated with an X-rated movie?

KITTEN: I didn't give a shit, because I was getting $2,000 a day. A lot of times, I do things just for money because I have to pay my rent and I'm very independent. And I'll tell you this, too. It got me more fans than you could believe...you'd be surprised how many people watch hard-core. Personally, I don't like it, but you make a lot of money doing hard-core. If I would've done the screwing in that film I would've gotten $5,000 a day. There was another one I did called "Bodacious Ta-tas" that Eddie Murphy is going to use a scene from in "Another 48 Hours." It's just this shot of me saying, "Oooh, I love to watch! I love to watch!"

JEWEL: And "Let's Talk Sex" is another hard-core movie you did?

"If I can hire myself, I'll give myself a part where I get killed in the first twenty minutes."

Melissa Prophet

A great number of actresses long for the security (and salaries) that can be found on the other side of the camera. Few can find a career there, but Melissa Prophet is an exception. Melissa's acting résumé boasts some of the upper class of B-films and finds her working now in A-movies. Today, she either acts in A-films or she chooses not to act; her success as a producer has given her that option. Born into a show business family, she clearly has had a good handle on the industry for her entire life and is now putting that knowledge to use.

JEWEL: You grew up here, didn't you?
MELISSA: In Los Angeles, right. My father is an entertainer, a lounge singer. His name is Johnny Prophet. He recorded nine records for Reprise Records. He still works Vegas, Reno, Tahoe. My mother was a burlesque dancer in the Honey Harlow, Lenny Bruce era. She was also a beauty queen. She was Miss Maryland...but they were just mom and dad.
JEWEL: How did they meet?
MELISSA: They were working together. My mother was dancing behind him at a show, I think it was at the Colony Club. She fell off the stage during rehearsal, so he helped her up and invited her to his beachhouse. The rest is history.
JEWEL: So you grew up in Los Angeles. What was that like?
MELISSA: Well, we travelled a lot because of my dad. So I went to school in Las Vegas and in Reno but we always kept a home in Rancho Palos Verdes.
JEWEL: Was that hard for you?
MELISSA: Actually, I loved it. It was always easy to make new friends and it was a new place to do my routine. I was a naughty puppy from the get-go. I was always the class clown, the loud mouth. I made friends very easily. I had a brother a year younger and a sister a year older and I'd go to them and introduce kids I'd met, to bring our families together...but by the time we were in high school, we pretty much stayed at Palos Verdes. Although I was expelled from six schools in the area. But it was never the schoolwork. I had the same attitude as the teachers: I just wanted to get home on Fridays. I was always really fast and really prepared, so I'd finish my work faster than everybody, and that's when I started horsing around. And I was loud and opinionated and got myself in trouble. It was never anything serious; I was just a fighter. My dad had two girls first, so before my brother was born my dad made up his mind that I was going to be his boy. So he taught me how to fight. I didn't just pull hair and

scratch like most girls, I fought. It was fun, it was power. I loved it.

JEWEL: When did you decide to drop the boxing career and get into acting?

MELISSA: Well, I won a beauty contest when I was seventeen. I was Miss San Pedro. My mother had wanted me to enter for years. She had won twenty-one beauty titles and my sister wouldn't even look at a camera. Anyway, right before Easter break that year, my best friend told me she was running for Miss Torrance. And I thought, "Oh, God, please." Then it turns out, she won. And she had this great picture of her being crowned with this tiara. I could just imagine the applause. And that was all my mom needed to convince me.

JEWEL: So you entered and you won...

MELISSA: Yeah, and it was weird because I beat out all these cheerleaders and all the good girls. So after being the bad girl, suddenly you're like...the beauty queen! After that I went onto win Miss Los Angeles and Miss California. I was third runner up in the Miss World Pageant and Miss USA. I won 14 first place trophies...It wasn't that I thought I was beautiful, it's just that I had a certain confidence that I got from my mother. It's the walk, it's the way you carry yourself...we had a theory that if you take twelve judges into a bar, every one will order something different. And that applies to who they want to be the beauty queen. So you have to take the time on your trip out on the ramp to make eye contact with each judge and show them what they want to see. My mother and I even researched the judges, found out their backgrounds.

With producer Robert Evans on the set of "Players" (1979)

JEWEL: So when did you burn out on the contest scene?

MELISSA: The minute it was over at the Miss USA pageant I knew I was finished. I was tired. My mom wanted me to go back, and so did the director for the Miss USA pageant. They wanted me to go back as Miss Nevada, but I said, "No way!" It was done. That chapter was finally closed.

JEWEL: Did you land any modeling contracts out of this?

MELISSA: I won modeling agency contracts, portfolios, a bunch of jewelry and luggage.

JEWEL: When did you make the transition into acting?

MELISSA: Actually, while I was still in high school I was acting in the school plays, like "South Pacific." It was my best girlfriend, Linda, who dragged me to all these things. She was the one who basically dragged me into Hollywood.

JEWEL: So what was your first Hollywood job?

MELISSA: I got a job working for Telly Savalas.

JEWEL: (laughs) How?

MELISSA: It was Linda...We were at Art Laboe's on Sunset Strip. They used to do this thing, "Live, from Hollywood, it's the Art Laboe Show!" It was Saturday night at midnight. Art Laboe was an old deejay who used to play my dad's records. So my girlfriend and I went up there as Miss Torrance and Miss San Pedro and talked to Art about being beauty queens. Then, as we were leaving for our cars, Linda starts saying, "It's Kojak! It's Kojak!" It was his first season and several other guys from the show came over to us and dragged us back into the studio because they were going to do an interview with Art. So we talked to Telly, who said he was looking for a girl Friday. I knew he was a ladies man, but I decided to do it. So I went to work for him in September, signing fan mail, "Who loves ya, baby?" He was literally getting tons of fan mail from women ages 8 to 80, telling him how sexy he was. I had a better Telly Savalas signature than he did. In fact, he used to say, "Hide the checkbooks!" I worked for him for three years, and I met a lot of people in the industry. And there were a lot of perks, because that show was the hottest show on television. Companies sent us all cars...I was driving an Eldorado Cadillac and a Jaguar, and I had my own parking space with my name on it at Universal Studios when I was only 17 and a half years old! I thought, "This is great."

JEWEL: Did Telly give you your first acting break?

MELISSA: He put me on his album cover and he put me in a CBS special he did. Then he finally gave me a job in a movie that he directed, that Howard Koch produced. It's called "Beyond Reason." I think it's on video now...But I never did any episodes of Kojak. He would set up auditions for me to be on the show, but I didn't go. I don't know why.

JEWEL: Okay, so after you left Telly, what did you do?

MELISSA: I did some TV shows like "Rosetti & Ryan," "Quark," "CHiPS" and little bit parts in other stuff.

JEWEL: How did you make the segue into features?

MELISSA: Well, a photographer calls me up — and at this point I am Miss California — and he asks me if I want to meet Robert Evans. Now, Robert Evans was, at the time, the king of Hollywood. He was this mogul. And I was always the kind of person who was fascinated and fixated with power figures. Well, he'd married Phyllis George the year before, so when this photographer calls, I go, "But isn't he married to Phyllis George?" And he says, "Not anymore..." So

I said, "Of course," and he tells me to show up at Robert's house that night for a screening. Well, I'm wearing this darling little tight white pants thing and a blue shirt. Anyway, I get there and did he have the spread...It's a beautiful home. And I liked him right away. So the photographer leaves and Robert and I just stayed there talking until midnight. But then the next day or so, I took off for Chicago.

JEWEL: Didn't you start dating him?

MELISSA: Well, I had a boyfriend who was living in Chicago, and after I came back from Chicago, I started dating Evans. We knew we weren't going to fall in love or anything, but I really liked him. And I thought he could help me...sure enough, he was doing a movie called "Players" with Ali McGraw and Dean-Paul Martin, and a young actor named Steve Guttenberg. And he said that there was a part I could play if I wanted. I never even had to audition. He just gave me the part. And I did it...I made nice money and got a great credit.

JEWEL: So what happened next?

MELISSA: Well I got the lead in a B-movie called "Van Nuys Blvd."

JEWEL: "Van Nuys Blvd." is kind of a cult film, isn't it?

MELISSA: Yeah, I guess so. But when I was growing up, people really did cruise the boulevard. So when I got the part, it was like, "Yeah, I know all about this." Plus, it was my first lead. It was a lot of fun. Bob even made the deal for me. He was real generous that way. So that whole thing happens, and while Bob was off doing "Urban Cowboy," I was in over in Europe with Adnan Khoshogi.

JEWEL: How did you meet him!?

MELISSA: Through my dad. We were at the Sands Hotel in Las Vegas where my dad was appearing and he introduced me to this man called "A.K." My dad had known him for years. He'd sing A.K. his favorite songs and get tipped $3,000. My dad thought this guy was *it!* So I met A.K. and ended up going over to Europe and visiting his family, which ended up being about a six-year trip. I guess I was his favorite girlfriend. We had a great relationship. We understood each other so well. I call that period of my life my six-year magic carpet ride.

JEWEL: What kind of life was it with him?

MELISSA: It was like a movie...there'd be days when I'd get my wake-up call and he'd ask what I wanted to do that day. And I'd say, "Oh, I don't know. I'm bored." Then, twenty minutes later, he'd call and say, "Okay, we'll get the plane and we're going to Marbella. Or we're going to the Canary Islands, or we're going to Monte Carlo..."

JEWEL: So you were living this kind of princess lifestyle, but what about your acting career?

MELISSA: A.K. was very good about sending me back whenever I had an audition. I'd be between say, Majorca and Cannes on his yacht in the middle of a storm, and he'd have the plane sent to Majorca so I could go back to L.A. for my audition...then I get to the airport and there would be a limo waiting. I mean, I'd arrive for these auditions in a limo! *(laughs)* The first year, I walked around with my mouth hanging open. But after that, it felt like that's what normal people did. Then pretty soon, it was like, "What do you mean the helicopter's not here yet?" I got really snitty. Or I'd say, "This servant said something! I'm going to move her to another villa!" A.K. just kind of convinced me that this lifestyle was my destiny.

JEWEL: How did A.K. get into movies? Were you involved in that?

MELISSA: We always used to joke about how rich he was...but he wanted more, and we talked about financing movies. Anyway, I'm flying to New York for Stan Dragoti's birthday party. And I'm flying on a commercial airline. Well, guess who's sitting next to me? Bob Evans. Now I hadn't seen him in a year or so, and he was looking for independent financing for "The Cotton Club." So we spent five hours on the plane talking about it, and if A.K. would be interested. Well, I met A.K. in Las Vegas about it and pitched the idea to him, saying this would be a great boot camp for me to learn producing. He just said, "Great. Go get him." So I brought Bob back to Las Vegas and he did his dog and pony show for A.K., who loved the idea. He thought it was a great investment, plus he wanted to help me. So he offered Bob $2.5 million as seed money, to develop the script. But Evans says, "No, I can get the money, myself." Then he left. But I remember it perfectly: We stood at the end of the driveway watching him leave and A.K. put his arms around me and says, "He'll be back." And like clockwork, two weeks later, he was back.

With Dean-Paul Martin in "Players" (1979)

JEWEL: Now what was your involvement in the deal?

MELISSA: I was set to be the Associate Producer, for good money...so Bob hires Mario Puzo to write the script and we have this big party for him in Las Vegas. And after that, they were going to have a meeting, because Bob wanted A.K. to step up and put in another $10 million. Well, A.K. agreed, but he wanted a partner...a studio, or a distributor. So they spent weeks trying to negotiate the deal. Bob and A.K. couldn't come to terms on who owned what portion of the film, so A.K. finally pulled out, even though he still owned 25% of the film. Anyway, Bob and I went around to everybody we knew trying to get the financing...we even tried Jerry Buss, who didn't want to do it. But there was some guy at the meeting who knew someone, who knew two guys that might want to to it.

JEWEL: Was this the Domeni brothers?

MELISSA: Yeah. They were in the oil business, the hotel business...really solid guys. So they put up, like, $38 million. The problem was, A.K. still owned

25% of the film for only a $2.5 million investment. The Domenis eventually agreed to buy him out, even though it cost them extra to do it.

JEWEL: Now during this time, did you do anything in the way of acting?

MELISSA: Yes. A.K. financed another movie called "Timewalker," and instead of taking a producer's credit, I took a co-starring role in it. Then I did another film called "Blame it on the Night" with Nick Mancuso. I helped raise the money for that one through some Texans, with a friend of mine, Gene Taft. There was another one over in Europe I did with David Niven, Art Carney and Maggie Smith called "Better Late than Never." After that there was "Looker" and "Melvin & Howard."

JEWEL: What were you in "Melvin & Howard"?

MELISSA: Remember the game show that Paul LeMat's wife goes on? Well, I was an "Easy Street" model.

JEWEL: What about "Invasion, U.S.A."?

MELISSA: Well I'd just lost the female lead in "Black Moon Rising" to Linda Hamilton. I'd also just finished "The Cotton Club" and had decided to return to acting. So when my agent called and said there was a Chuck Norris picture, I said, "Of course."

JEWEL: And did you have to actually audition for this?

MELISSA: Yeah, I went through three or four auditions. But it was a lot of fun. Chuck was such a nice guy. We were in Atlanta and Miami...when you travel with Chuck and his pack, it's like high action all the time. They wanted me in all the stunt scenes, even though there was a stunt woman for me.

JEWEL: Weren't you scared?

MELISSA: You don't even know...there was this car chase scene that took about three weeks to film, and they had this harness thing on me that was hooked to the floorboard of the car. During the chase, I'm supposed to pull this girl off this moving car and save her while I'm hanging out the side of my car...well, after we'd done it three times, I got up and went to the bathroom. And when I came back, I forgot to buckle myself back in. Just when they yell, "Action!" I realize this and think, "God, what would've happened if you didn't catch that?"

JEWEL: What was "The Killing Touch"? I've never seen that one.

MELISSA: That was just this crazy little movie I did about four women training for the Olympics that all get killed. I got impaled with a javelin by Sally Kirkland.

JEWEL: You haven't done a lot of nudity in your films, but how do you feel about it?

MELISSA: If it goes with the storyline, that's fine. But if it's exploitation, then forget it.

JEWEL: What about that recent *Playboy* article and spread?

MELISSA: During "Invasion, U.S.A." they ran a small photo of me in the back of the magazine and I ran into the editor afterwards at this Christmas party. And she said to me, "You were Miss California, you're an actress, you're a producer...would you be interested in doing a layout called *Diary of a Hollywood Starlet*, where you could sort of have fun with it all?" Well I had turned down offers from *Playboy* and *Penthouse* when I was younger, but I figured, why not? And it wasn't sleazy at all. It was very professional.

JEWEL: Speaking of that, were you ever hit on by agents or producers?

MELISSA: I wasn't really a target. I mean, they go after girls that can be taken advantage of. Sure, I got hit on, and if I didn't, I'd be worried! But most of those guys knew it wasn't going to work with me. There's a million girls they can sleep with, but you have to have something else to offer...I'll tell you, this town is a machine. It's business. But a lot of it is people being involved with people. It's friendships and preparation all tied in with luck.

JEWEL: What do you see for yourself in the future?

MELISSA: Well, just recently, I got a part in a Martin Scorsese film called "Goodfellas" starring Robert DeNiro and Ray Liotta...I played a gangster's wife. It wasn't a real big part but, hey, if I stopped acting today, I would be happy. Martin Scorsese was the best.

JEWEL: Are you going to ever return to producing?

MELISSA: As a matter of fact, I am producing what you would call a B-movie right now. It's a female version of "Dirty Harry," starring Vanity. We've got a $7 million budget. I've also hired myself as an actress in the movie...the bottom line is, I don't have Debra Winger's career. And I know that. So I think I'm just going to produce movies and act for people I've worked for before. Or if I can hire myself, I'll give myself a part where I get killed in the first twenty minutes. That way, the whole movie's not resting on my shoulders. You know, I think I'm probably better at producing than acting...and I make better money.

With Chuck Norris in "Invasion, U.S.A." (1985)

"It wasn't until I saw the screening that I realized what kind of movie it really was."

Linnea Quigley

At any given time, there is always one actress whose prolific work — and high-profile, low-budget appearances — earns her the title of "Queen of the B's." At the moment, Linnea Quigley is the reigning monarch in this field. Other actresses are agog (and, many, envious) at how many films per year she adds to her credit list. When *Variety*, the show business bible, toted up the number of film appearances per year for recent movie stars, the name of Linnea Quigley was at the tip-top of the low budget category. Perhaps the workingest actress in all of Hollywood, Linnea has built up an impressive cult following of horror and s-f fans who queue up for hours when she is doing a personal appearance.

JEWEL: I hear you dropped your last name.

LINNEA: I'm using just Linnea for the comedies and that sort of thing. Then I use Linnea Quigley for the horror films. It was something my management just kind of did...but I like Quigley. I think I'm going to keep it. *(laughs)*

JEWEL: *(laughs)* So where do the Quigleys come from?

LINNEA: Davenport, Iowa, where we lived for eighteen years. Then I came to California with my parents. My father's a chiropractor and a psychologist. My mother's a housewife.

JEWEL: Did you dream about the movie business back in Davenport?

LINNEA: It wasn't until I started working at a health spa here in Los Angeles that I heard how everyone was working in the business. So I thought I could maybe get into TV.

JEWEL: How old were you at the time?

LINNEA: I was eighteen...but I didn't move out here to become an actress, I just wanted to be someplace warm.

JEWEL: Were you the All-American girl type back in Davenport?

LINNEA: *(laughs)* I wanted to be, but I was too shy. Once I tried out for cheerleader, but I didn't make it. I wasn't popular at all. Guys used to line on both sides of the second story at school and drop books on my head. I was terrorized, so I hated going to school. They called me names and stuff...and there were race riots all the time, and the black girls would drag me down the halls by my hair.

JEWEL: *(amazed)* This was in Davenport, Iowa?

LINNEA: Yeah, it was just a really bad time to be in Davenport. But that wasn't really the reason I wanted to leave. It was more that I was shy and it would've been harder to change there and be accepted.

JEWEL: So you're out here living with your parents...what was your first

step towards becoming an actress?

LINNEA: It was really depressing because I didn't know anybody and I couldn't drive on the freeways...my big ambition was just to work at a spa. That was really exciting to me. It was like, "Wow!" Anyway, working at this spa was how I got into nude modelling, because these other girls that worked there took me to this agent...I was so naive. This guy was, like, the nicest guy, and he said it was just going to be a little figure modelling, maybe some bathing suit stuff. I was like, *(coy)* "Okay..."

JEWEL: So when you were asked to do your first nude session, how did you feel?

LINNEA: I was terrified. But I thought if I said "No," maybe it was just me, that there was something wrong with me. I mean, everybody else there was doing it and this agent was, like, "Oh, it's fine!" So I figured it wasn't so bad. Plus, they paid, like, $100 a day and that was a lot of money then...but I still felt horrible.

JEWEL: How did you get into B-movies?

LINNEA: All of a sudden this agent started sending me out for little bit parts in B-movies, like a shower scene or something.

JEWEL: Then you, what, just started making friends with the producers?

LINNEA: Yeah.

JEWEL: And that led to bigger parts?

LINNEA: Yeah, but because it was new to me, I didn't mind just having one line. Eventually I started taking acting classes so I could get into it more.

JEWEL: Would you tell your friends about these movies where you'd just take off your clothes and maybe have one line?

LINNEA: At first I did, because it was kind of exciting. But then I went to some of them and I didn't like it...my friends were pretty shocked, but after a while, for me, it became pretty normal.

JEWEL: What were some of these earlier films you did?

LINNEA: "Stone Cold Dead," where I was in a shower and got shot. Richard Crenna and Paul Williams were in that one. Then I did, "Fairy Tales," where I played a topless Sleeping Beauty for Charlie Band at Empire. I did a horrible movie called "Don't Go Near the Park," which had nudity, but also gave me a few lines. Then there was "Summer Camp" with Mark Borde...more nudity. Eventually, I progressed on to "Graduation Day."

JEWEL: That's right. You played the slutty girl in the class. Now, were people getting to know you, or were you still having to audition?

LINNEA: No, I still had to audition. Mark Borde told me about "Graduation Day" and recommended me, but I got the part because the actress they had hired refused to take off her top.

JEWEL: It didn't bother you to have to keep taking off your top?

LINNEA: It didn't really seem like, with those kind of films, that there was an option.

JEWEL: You sure had to take it off in "Return of the Living Dead."

LINNEA: Yeah, you're lucky you didn't have to be a zombie in that one! *(laughs)* They had to put a full body prothesis on me and when the extras had to eat me, they got a little carried away and overzealous. I don't know what comes over people.

JEWEL: Was that film emotionally draining for you?

LINNEA: I think it was the second week, the only day they didn't have rain machines, and it was really humid. I'd just done my tombstone dance and it was six in the morning...I remember practically passing out. Somebody had to drive me home.

JEWEL: Considering that you've been killed every way possible: beaten to death, shot, stabbed, mutilated, ripped apart...do you feel any certain sensation when you see your death scenes on screen?

LINNEA: Not really. Most of the films I've done have just been fun black comedies...the only film that really bothers me is "Silent Night, Deadly Night," because it is more a slasher film than most of the stuff I do. It was just too real, having a deranged Santa Claus.

JEWEL: Were you concerned about the moral implications of that film, especially on kids, before you took the part?

"Return of the Living Dead" (1985)

LINNEA: Going into it I thought it was just going to be another stupid movie. I didn't spend time going through the whole script because I just had one or two scenes and I didn't care. It wasn't until I saw the screening that I realized what kind of movie it really was.

JEWEL: In retrospect, does all the violence you've been associated with in your movies bother you?

LINNEA: If I did it all the time, that would be horrible. But the roles I've done recently haven't been just having sex and getting killed. I've even saved a few people...I ususally turn down slasher pictures.

JEWEL: Didn't you do one of the "Nightmare on Elm Street" movies?

LINNEA: My husband [special effects expert Steve Johnson] got me that part...It was just, like, they painted us up and we were stretching out of Freddy's chest at the end of the movie. It was nothing, but they gave me a good credit.

JEWEL: So let's go over your credits...

LINNEA: Well, there was "Hollywood Chainsaw Hookers," "Sorority Babes in the Slime Ball Bowl-O-Rama," "Creepazoids"...

JEWEL: Tell me about "Creepazoids." I never saw that one.

LINNEA: That was after I'd pretty much stopped acting for a year...I'd done "Return of the Living Dead," and then went to Mexico and did "Treasure of the Moon Goddess," where I played a punk rock singer who gets kidnaped by these natives that think she's the moon goddess. It was a big thing for me, because it was comedy and I was happy about that. There was no nudity; it was terrific. But by the time I got back, I was just burned out. I had to get away from it all.

JEWEL: So how did you spend your time off?

LINNEA: I did go-go dancing...you just dance and serve drinks and get tips. It was okay.

JEWEL: Didn't that feel like a big step down from just starring in a comedy?

LINNEA: Not really. I didn't like doing it necessarily, but it was so nice just to be treated like a normal person. No interviews, no auditions...you just go in there and work four hours, get money. It was fine. The place was called "Hollywood A-Go-Go." After about five months, though, I got sick of it. Then Dave Dakota called and said he was doing his second film, "Creepazoids." It's about these six people that are in the army and hide out from acid rain in this shelter, but there's aliens in there and they have to fight them.

JEWEL: Did "Creepazoids" renew your interest in acting?

LINNEA: Yeah, it did. Mostly because there wasn't an audition and it was just working with people who would call you up and say, "Here's the script, here's the schedule, we'll shoot in two weeks."

JEWEL: It sounds like the rejection got to you...did you take it personally?

LINNEA: There was this one commercial audition...I'd just come from a Pepsi commercial where they had us in shorts and t-shirts, so I went right down the street to this audition for a waitress in a Sure deodorant ad. And this casting lady looks at me and says, *(nasty voice)* "I can't take you in there looking like that! Don't you have a waitress uniform?" It was so ridiculous. I just said "No!" and walked out. I couldn't understand what the difference was between shorts and a short skirt for an audition. It was so stupid.

JEWEL: What did you do after "Creepazoids"?

LINNEA: "Night of the Demons," which I almost didn't do because they wanted teenagers and I was twenty-six at the time.

JEWEL: Then you did "...Chainsaw Hookers," and "Sorority Babes..." And you were getting a lot of press. In fact, I saw you in *Premiere* magazine...

LINNEA: My P.R. people got me that, and from there it kind of snowballed...reporters started calling me out of the blue.

JEWEL: Did you finally feel successful?

LINNEA: I was still on an unsteady beat, but I was feeling more in the groove.

JEWEL: I suppose you were getting a lot of fan letters.

LINNEA: Yeah...about four a day. And I write them back, too. I also go to a lot of conventions, like I just went to this Fangoria Convention where I can meet the fans.

JEWEL: Any fans ever go a little over the edge?

LINNEA: Only two, and one was spawned by the TV show "The Reporters" that I did. This guy had no idea the movies I'd done. He'd just seen me on TV and found my parents' number through the directory and got my fan club address and wrote this really weird stuff. He even had the gall to ask my parents if he came out to California, could he sleep on their couch? *(laughs)*

JEWEL: After the Rebecca Schaeffer murder, doesn't that kind of thing scare you?

LINNEA: It does scare my husband, but I think that B-movie fans are mostly nice and sedate. It's the people that watch a lot of TV that are the most frightening.

JEWEL: So you have an official fan club, then?

LINNEA: The people who did my P.R. opened one a while ago, but I never saw any of the letters that came in. So I decided to make one more personal and do it myself...I send out a bumper sticker and a color photo and a newsletter, plus a picture of me and my dogs for their wallets.

JEWEL: How do you feel about not getting paid what mainstream actors do?

LINNEA: When *Premiere* printed what I was making, I got real mad. And after that I started demanding more and I found out that they would pay me what I wanted, because on low budget B-movies, they needed my name to sell the product. I got really mad there for a while. Some of these people I thought were my friends...then you find out they're screwing you.

JEWEL: What about making the leap into mainstream films?

LINNEA: Right now my goal is co-producing projects I want to see made. Like I did "Murder Weapon," which was just released a few months ago, and "The Girl I Want." And the deal was, I'd get what I always make on the films, but the other producer gave me a percentage of tape sales.

JEWEL: So you're getting more involved on the business side?

LINNEA: Exactly, and I feel like that's the best way to help out other people, too.

JEWEL: On the topic of helping others, what do you see as your personal cause?

LINNEA: Animal Rights. In fact, I donated a percentage of my tapes sales of "Murder Weapon" to P.E.T.A. That's what I'm most involved in, animal abuse: people wearing furs, laboratory animals, eating meat...I'm a vegetarian and I try not to buy anything made of real leather.

JEWEL: Is there anything you would like to change about your life?

LINNEA: I kind of look at it like, everything I've done has got me to where I am now. And I wouldn't want to change anything or that might screw up where I am now. What I went through made me what I am now. I never wanted a sugar-coated life.

"I jiggled an awful lot, but I kept my shirt on."

Jewel Shepard

When my editor insisted that I had to subject myself to the same cross-examination as all the others here, I asked a friend of mine to do the honors with the tape recorder and to edit the interview. Here is what resulted...

INTERVIEWER: Let's start with your childhood, where you were born...

JEWEL: Childhood for me was a very difficult, very painful existence. I was born in Flatbush, New York, but my mother and father were immigrants. My mother is British...she came from a totally different set of ideals; my father was of both Chinese and Portuguese descent, which makes me Bucanese. My mother won a trip on TWA to Japan and the man who would become my father was the tour guide there because he spoke English and, before they knew it, they were getting married in Tokyo. It was a strange marriage...a marriage of opposites. After I was born, my father didn't stick around much.

INTERVIEWER: British mother...Chinese and Portuguese father...they marry in Japan, have a kid in Brooklyn...

JEWEL: Yeah. (laughs) We were all over the place. My mother always kept moving, always figuring that the next locale would make a better life. We moved all through the South. I was mostly raised in North Carolina, but every so often, my mother would move us to the West Coast for the warmer climate...then back to the South...then back here again. I spent one semester out here attending Santa Monica High School and it was the longest I ever stayed in one school — a whole six months, I believe. Periodically, my mother would decide she couldn't handle raising a child and I would be put into some foster home for a time. One of my happier memories was of this farm in Pleasanton, California. I learned how to ride a horse, I learned all about farms...but, most of all, I learned some different ideas from what my mother had been teaching me. I started to be a little more independent.

INTERVIEWER: When did you start to think about being in show business?

JEWEL: I don't know for sure. When I was eight, I was hit by a car and I was in traction for six months. I spent a lot of the time fantasizing, thinking about what I wanted out of my life. I fantasized about being anybody but who I was.

INTERVIEWER: And, during this time, your mother was coming in and out of your life?

JEWEL: Every so often, she would reclaim me from whatever foster home I was in at the time and she would start again to indoctrinate me with her beliefs, the things she wanted to teach me.

INTERVIEWER: Any luck?

Me...in more innocent times.

JEWEL: I don't think she realized that she had forfeited that right, the first time she put me in a foster home and I was exposed to other ideas. Like, she wanted me to listen to "Madame Butterfly" and "La Boheme" and, in the meantime, I had discovered R&B, rhythm-and-blues music, and started a record collection. During this time, we were so poor that I used to have the school bus stop in front of a nice house down the block because I didn't want the other kids to see where we lived. Finally, I ran away from home. I ended up in Juvenile Hall and my mother, for all intents and purposes, disowned me.

INTERVIEWER: What was it like in Juvenile Hall?

JEWEL: Depressing. I was placed in with a girl who'd stabbed her parents. The thing is, you wind up having to be independent. Like, I realized that I was responsible for myself. I couldn't blame my mother, I couldn't wait for someone to help me. I had to be 110% responsible for my own life.

INTERVIEWER: So at one point did you set your sights on show business?

JEWEL: While I was in Juvenile Hall, I started reading. I read everything I could get my hands on and most of it was movie magazines. Right there was when I decided I was going to make something of myself; that I was going to have money and never be in that position again.

INTERVIEWER: When did you get out of there?

JEWEL: When I was sixteen, I was emancipated. By law, they have to do that. I hitchhiked down to Hollywood and I stayed with two friends I'd made when my mother and I were living here before, Emilio Estevez and Martin Sheen. They took care of me for a while, while I got on my feet.

INTERVIEWER: What was the first step into the business?

JEWEL: Emilio sent me to see an agent he knew. They said there was no way they could handle me with no experience.

INTERVIEWER: Did that discourage you?

JEWEL: I was undaunted. There was nothing that was going to stop me from achieving my dream of becoming a star. I then went to another agent who looked at my pictures — and, believe me, we're talking about rotten pictures — and he sent me on a call for "Charlie's Angels." This was back in the seventies, where you had blue eye-shadow and hip-hugger jeans and halter-tops...it was quite a fashion statement. I didn't get the job, but I felt I'd gotten close...I felt that, at any moment, I could break through. Well, that moment didn't come for many years.

INTERVIEWER: Did you feel like you were a part of the seventies' culture?

JEWEL: I did when I saw a movie that changed my life. I went and saw "Saturday Night Fever" and it changed my whole perception on the world. I became that whole spandex, see-thru blouse kind of girl with the coke spoon hanging around the neck. And it's amazing how the movies can define a time period and help you know what's expected of you. It was a time period when sexual scripts were being implied on the TV and played out on the movie screens and suddenly, every film that was casting was about teen-age sexuality and coming-of-age.

INTERVIEWER: How did you start in movies?

JEWEL: I started off as a non-union extra, getting twenty-five bucks a day — sometimes less and sometimes, for a sixteen hour day — and I worked up to other things. Then I was a girl who said one line, then I was a girl who said two lines, then I was a girl who said five lines...

INTERVIEWER: Mostly in films about teen-age sexuality and sexual awakening?

JEWEL: That's what was out there. That's what was casting and a lot it was just a matter of survival and paying the rent. In actuality, I went from being a girl who said one line and took off her top to being a girl who said two lines and took off her top to being a girl who said five lines...

INTERVIEWER: ...and took off her top.

JEWEL: That was the only way to build up film experience. I went to U.C.L.A. and I went to Berkeley. I paid my way through by dancing. At the time, it was

My first professional modelling job. For STREET-RODDERS Magazine.
That's automotive designer George Barris driving the Geoffreymobile.

119

dancing...bikini dancing and topless dancing. And nude dancing was just breaking the horizon. It was a painful experience to have to take off your clothes, just to keep food on the table, but I didn't have anyone or anything else at that moment.

INTERVIEWER: When did you finally get your S.A.G. card?

JEWEL: On a "Charlie's Angels," of all things. At a later date.

INTERVIEWER: What other shows did you do?

JEWEL: "Starsky and Hutch," a few others. We're talking about one-line parts here, playing hookers, playing little debutante girls. My first theatrical film was "The Junk Man," an H.B. Halicki production. He had just finished "Gone in Sixty Seconds" the year before and this was the sequel starring Hoyt Axton and Lynda Day George. I got a few lines and a credit and that was, like, "Wow, a movie." I went to the premiere and I was so impressed.

INTERVIEWER: When did you do "Zapped"?

JEWEL: That was my second film but I wasn't fortunate enough to have any lines in that. I was just fortunate enough to have my shirt zapped off by Scott Baio.

INTERVIEWER: How did you feel about doing that?

JEWEL: It was kind of embarrassing. I didn't want to be known as the girl who took off her clothes in movies and I wasn't really proud of my body at the time. I felt my tits were kind of floppy. Then, in "My Tutor," I played Matt Lattanzi's dream girl that he sees in a phone booth and, of course, my top did come off...

My first professional head shot.

INTERVIEWER: What a surprise.

JEWEL: Then I was real lucky. I got an agent and, virtually the same week, he sent me on a call for a movie called "Hollywood Hot Tubs." Mark Borde hired me and I played Crystal Landers — this daffy little valley girl — daughter of a woman who ran a hot tub company. The film did real well, for the kind of film it was, and it gave me moments to actually act, plus I kept my shirt on. I jiggled an awful lot, but I kept my shirt on.

INTERVIEWER: About this time, you did "Return of the Living Dead," written and directed by Dan O'Bannon.

JEWEL: I met him...(laughs) through friends. He knew I was working in a strip joint and he used to say to me, "Jewel, one of these days, I will get you out of there and give you a part in a movie if I ever

get that chance." And he was true to his word. I mean, I had to audition for it but he gave me the chance and he was pulling for me all the way. I think I did seven auditions. But he's a great man and I felt so good being in that movie.

INTERVIEWER: Was there nudity involved in this role?

JEWEL: Strange thing about that. Dan said to me, "I'd like you to play the role of Trash...you'd have to take off all your clothes." I guess, understandably, he knew I'd worked in a strip joint, he figured I'd have no objection to something like that but I said, "Dan, I just can't. I've done it...I've done topless things my whole life. I want to have my clothes on." And he said, "Okay, there's this punk rock role I'm writing. Would you like to play that?"

INTERVIEWER: You met Linnea Quigley on that film?

JEWEL: I met her again. Linnea and I had worked together a few years earlier on this thing called "Sweet Dreams" for SelecTV and we both had to take off our tops in that. So now, here we were on Dan's movie, working together again. She got to play Trash and when I saw what she went through, I was so grateful that she was doing it. She was better emotionally-equipped to deal with that role than I would have been. So it all worked out for the best...and the movie became a cult classic. To this day, people stop me and say, "God, that was such a great movie."

INTERVIEWER: How did you feel, working with a director like Dan?

JEWEL: It was great. I had worked with so many directors who were more like traffic cops. You know, they get their master shot, they get their medium shot, they get their close-ups and that's it. Not a word about acting or motivation or who the people are in the scene. On that kind of film, if it's done on time and it cuts together, they've done their job. Working with Dan was so much better. He made me feel like an actress.

INTERVIEWER: Was there a down-side to the film for you?

JEWEL: Just this: I played a punk rocker so I had my hair short and it was blue and red...and nobody recognized me. I would walk up and down movie theater aisles, hoping to get recognized, and nobody did. And none of my friends from school recognized me, either.

INTERVIEWER: How did you get from there to "Knots Landing"?

JEWEL: I met a director who was about to direct a segment of the show and he said, "I want to use you in a role." I wound up playing Gary Ewing's lover for a season there. Then, right as that was ending, I got this film called "Going Undercover" with Chris Lemmon and Lea Thompson. I really was getting psyched because here was another real movie, a big-budget movie, and I didn't have to take off my clothes or anything.

INTERVIEWER: So, by this point, you were getting something of a reputation...

JEWEL: I guess so. Mark Borde called me and asked me to be in this film he was doing called "Party Camp," playing a sexpot. I tried to do something different but, through the edits, I ended up not quite pulling off the character idea that I had planned...so that's another one of those movies I have to sort of live down.

INTERVIEWER: Did you get that because you'd worked for Borde on "Hollywood Hot Tubs"?

JEWEL: Yes. The heads of Lightning Pictures for Vestron saw "Hollywood Hot Tubs" and, when they did "Party Camp" with Mark, they asked him to get

With Catherine Mary Stewart in "Scenes from the Goldmine." (Photo: Joe Mineau)

me for that film. Then, the people at the Playboy Channel saw "H.H.T." and they asked the producer of a film they were funding called "Christina" to get me for the lead. I played Christina VonBelle, the richest girl in the world, which I found rather a crock because I hadn't had a lot of experience in having a lot of money. But it was all about the jet set world so I wound up going to Europe and getting kidnapped by ninja women and having every man I saw...I got to shoot in London and Paris and Spain.

INTERVIEWER: Did the crew all speak English?

JEWEL: Oh, God, no. Most of the cast and crew spoke French or Spanish and it was just the most confusing thing because they would learn their lines phonetically in English, but not very well. And, as if acting in that situation wasn't hard enough, we were shooting in the dead of winter, but the script called for it to be summer...so I had to run around in all these brief little things and I was freezing. The lab that was developing the film would call up and say, "Is she supposed to look blue like that?"

INTERVIEWER: The film was redubbed, wasn't it?

123

JEWEL: Yeah. After they edited it, they called me up to fly back to Europe because they were going to redub the whole thing. Unfortunately, I was shooting a picture here and they said, "We can't wait for you" and they got someone else to do my voice. So, in addition to all the other things I went through, when I see the movie, there's someone else's voice coming out of my mouth.

INTERVIEWER: Yet another movie to live down?

JEWEL: Yeah.

INTERVIEWER: Tell us about some films you liked.

JEWEL: Well, I did this film that Jackie Kong directed called "The Under-achievers." I played a spaced-out Star Trekkie and I got to work with Becky LeBeau again. Becky was in "Hollywood Hot Tubs" with me so we were old friends. But I'll tell you a film I really liked. I did "Scenes from the Gold Mine" in which I got to play Catherine Mary Stewart's best friend. It was a rock-and-roll movie which featured Timothy B. Schmit from the Eagles and John Ford Coley and I got to work with all these rock people...and Melissa Ethridge. She said one line in the movie and wrote some of the songs and I remember asking her, "What do you do?" and she said, "I'm a songwriter." I said, "Wow, that's a very tough business. I hope you do well in it." And she said, "Yeah, I hope I do, too." It was another good movie.

INTERVIEWER: How do you feel when you look over your body of work?

JEWEL: Well, you know, I look at the list and I say to myself, "Hey, I've done some good movies. I've worked with some good people." But, other times, you can get so down on yourself because you're not progressing, not getting on to the

A poster signing at Hollywood Book and Poster Co. reunites cast and crew from "Return of the Living Dead." In back: Production Designer Bil Stout; In front, left to right: Mark Venturini, Jewel, Miguel Nunez, Linnea Quigley, Director Dan O'Bannon (with face in poster), Brian Peck, Unidentified Publicity Man, Thom Matthews.

big films that everyone hears about. I know I shouldn't look down on what I've done, but actors are such neurotic people. It's real easy to not feel good about yourself at times.

INTERVIEWER: Now, one day you got a call about "Hollywood Hot Tubs II"?

JEWEL: Yes. Mark Borde phoned up and said, "We can use your character of Crystal and have her grow up. You and your mom can be running this little hot tub club." It seemed so silly to me to do a sequel..."Ten years later...the sequel that all the world demanded!" But it was fun and now it shows incessantly on cable. And it turned out okay. I'm proud of it, in a way, what with having to change Crystal from the valley girl attitude she had in the first one and at the start of this picture, and to have her grow up during the sequel.

INTERVIEWER: Did you ever worry about being typecast as a valley girl?

JEWEL: It's always a problem. I like doing the broad films, the teen comedies, but the frustrating part is that the serious films — the ones that require real acting — just don't get seen much. Tons of people have seen me in the "Hollywood Hot Tubs" movies. Almost no one has seen me in "Scenes from the Gold Mine." I know I can do other things. I've studied acting. I can do serious parts.

INTERVIEWER: It would seem like Hollywood is so big...

JEWEL: It isn't. It may look that way from the outside, but inside, it's a very small little fishbowl. And if you're outside that fishbowl, it's damn hard to get in.

INTERVIEWER: Have you ever felt like giving up?

JEWEL: More times than I like to think. I think everyone does. But the minute you give up, you've lost. You don't lose until you give up. I know there are more films in my future and better films...I just kind of thought they'd get here sooner.

INTERVIEWER: In the interviews you've done for this book, have you heard or felt the same thing from other actresses?

JEWEL: Felt more than heard, but yes. We're all bucking some formidable obstacles and I think all that most of us ever have going for ourselves is that drive to succeed. Sometimes, the film you thought was going to do it for you doesn't turn out so great or your best scene winds up being edited out — which has happened to me, a couple of times. Sometimes, it's a long stretch between auditions and, sometimes, you don't get called for the auditions because you're the Chainsaw Girl to them or the Swinging Cheerleader to them and they figure, if you can do that other kind of film, you can't do the more serious movie. That's when it gets *really* frustrating — when you can't even get in the door to audition and show them what you can do. A lot of us have done the male fantasy roles for the male producers and the male audiences, and I don't think we should be penalized for it. I think we should all get the chance to show the industry what else we can do *besides* wear a wet t-shirt and dismember bodies.

INTERVIEWER: Is there anything you think you can do to communicate that to the industry?

JEWEL: Well, maybe I can put together a book about it...

"So I showed up with a black wig because Goldie didn't want someone else with blonde hair in a big role"

P.J. Soles

It was in a cheapo Roger Corman film with an impossibly-short shooting schedule that P.J. Soles first got noticed by many. Playing Riff Randall, fan *numero uno* of the rock group, the Ramones, she helped bring "Rock 'n' Roll High School" to a high level of attention. The film stands as a splendid example of how a witty script and personable leads can triumph over a decided lack of budget. Films funded by producer-entrepeneur Roger Corman have never been noted for good roles for actors, particularly for women, but the reviews of this one were unanimously enchanted with P.J.. As discussed below, she usually has worked that fine line between B-movies and the A-variety, often in films that began as the latter and slipped over into the upper scale. "Carrie" and "Halloween," for example, both started life as mere horror potboilers but distinguished themselves to become successful (and much imitated) hits. Obviously, actors such as P.J. are a key reason.

JEWEL: Does P.J. stand for anything interesting?

P.J.: Just Pamela Jane, but I have very strange beginnings. My parents met in Frankfurt, Germany. My mother was married before, but her first husband was killed in the war, so while she was over there she met my father, who had just been released from a concentration camp.

JEWEL: Why was he in a concentration camp?

P.J.: He was with the Dutch Underground...when he was nineteen he was caught in his mother's attic and arrested for helping the Jews escape out of Holland. He was sent to what's called a work camp, and when he was released, it was at the base my mother was visiting to see the place where her first husband died.

JEWEL: Did they move back to the U.S.?

P.J.: No. My mother helped my father get a job as a stockboy with an insurance company in Frankfurt. But because he spoke so many languages, they sent him to Casablanca to open a new office. So I've lived there and in Venezuela. I even went to high school in Brussels. I didn't come to the States until I was eighteen.

JEWEL: Being raised internationally, it must've been hard to root yourself somewhere...

P.J.: It was sort of weird...I felt like an outsider. But I still felt at home in each of the countries because my mother made sure we always lived in normal neighborhoods and ate the local foods.

JEWEL: Are you an only child?

P.J.: I had an older brother by two years, but he died in a private plane crash in '78. I also have a younger brother by seven years.

JEWEL: What were the pros and cons of growing up abroad?

P.J.: I suppose it made me imaginative...it made me open to just about any situation. I definitely feel that all mankind is equal from being exposed to such diverse cultures.

JEWEL: Did you see a lot of movies when you were growing up?

P.J.: Not really. We had TV from 6 to 8 at night, and that was mostly news. We did have one cartoon called "Cantinflas." He's like the Jerry Lewis of South America...and yet, I was always very into poetry and dramatics. I was always in all the school plays.

JEWEL: You must have stuck out in Venezuela, being so causcasian-looking.

P.J.: Yeah...but we had what are called International Schools that were for everybody not from the native country. Half the classes were taught in English, the other half in Spanish. And the drama teachers were mostly from England, which made for very classical training...but I never really thought of acting as something you could pursue as a career. It was just for fun.

JEWEL: Where did you go to college?

P.J.: My mother wanted me to go to a small girl's college in Istanbul, where my parents were moving, but I wanted to go the States, which I'd always heard so much about from the Americans we met all around the world. Also, my father thought America was the greatest place in the world because they liberated the concentration camps and won WWII. So anyway, I went to Briarcliff College in New York. I went to New York City with a girlfriend from Briarcliff and she was going out with a guy who took us to Joe Allen's, which is where the people from The Actor's Studio hang out. And they were all talking about plays, which was very familiar to me. Then Joshua White invited me to come and see a showcase at the studio, which was great. And while I was there, I checked the job board and found a summer job working the spotlights. So they let me do that and audit classes at the same time. I remember Scott Glenn and Joanna Miles were performing in something together, so all summer I worked the spotlight for them.

JEWEL: So when did you get your first break?

P.J.: Joshua said, "You're really nice looking. If you want to start making big money, you should let me introduce you to my sister's agent so you can do commercials." And that's all how it happened, in this three-month span during the summer.

JEWEL: So what did the agent say when he met you?

P.J.: When I told him that I was from all these different countries, he said, "What!? You look like you're from California!" But he sent me out on a Crisco commercial that first week and I got it. He also got me into modeling because I had this California look...and they were very surprised that I could actually talk, let alone act, because this was before all the big models started acting.

JEWEL: What was your first dramatic acting role?

P.J.: I got a part on the soap opera, "Love is a Many Splendored Thing," which I did for nine months. Then after that, I decided to move on to film and television...I had already auditioned for several pilots like "The Partridge Family" and this will tell you how naive I was: It was the final audition for the show and Susan Dey was there and they get me on tape and ask me if I would like to go to California? Now I had no idea what getting on this show would mean to my career, so I said, "Well, I don't know if I'm really ready. I really love New York. I'm having such a great time here!" Then they asked me what I thought of the part and I said, "Oh, it's all right, but I think that girl *(Susan Dey)* out there would be perfect. She's really cute." *(laughs)* They must've thought I was a nut!

JEWEL: So when did you finally make it out here?

P.J.: I got married to Steven Soles, who's a singer and songwriter. We were married four years but our schedules just didn't work out. He would do late night gigs and I'd be up at six in the morning for modeling shoots. We parted friends, but I decided to move out here after that, which was around '75. My New York agent had set me up with modeling and talent agents so when I got here, I had them waiting for me. But I didn't really get into the modeling scene out here. It's much different than in New York. I decided to concentrate on acting.

JEWEL: What was your first big film audition?

P.J.: My agent sent me to a joint casting session with Brian DePalma and George Lucas. Brian was looking for girls for "Carrie," and George was casting "Star Wars." They wanted to see every girl in town. Of course, they weren't such big names back then. They just asked us where we were from and what we'd done...then, two weeks later, my agent called and told me to go to Brian's house where he was having a script read-through. For three weeks in a row, this group of ten kids all read every part in the script, over and over.

"Rock 'n' Roll High School" (1979)

With Jamie Lee Curtis in "Halloween" (1978)

JEWEL: So all of you were discovered at this cattle call?

P.J.: Yeah, and Sissy Spacek's story was amazing. Her husband, Jack Fisk, was set to be the art director, and he kept telling Brian to consider his wife, but Brian said he already had too many people. Then he finally met her at the screen testing and let her read. Well, she just blew them away.

JEWEL: What about John Travolta?

P.J.: At the time we were filming, he hadn't got hot yet. It was that summer after the movie came out that "Welcome Back, Kotter" really took off.

JEWEL: So what character did you play?

P.J.: I played Norma, the one with the red cap. I wanted to play the Nancy Allen role, but for whatever reason, Brian wanted me to play her friend, instead. The funny thing about the hat was that I'd worn the red hat to all the auditions, so when the screen test came around and I wasn't wearing it, Brian asked me to get it. After that, I wore it in every scene. It was a nice touch.

JEWEL: Why do you think you were chosen over the thousands of other girls that auditioned?

P.J.: I think probably because I had a different background from the other girls, who had grown up in Iowa, or wherever. I think I just had an edge to me, or maybe a spark of wisdom.

JEWEL: Did you realize that "Carrie" was going to be such a big movie?

P.J.: Not at all. I don't think any of us did. We were all getting S.A.G. minimum, which I think was, like, $652 a week. To us it was a lot of money, but we had no idea...it opened a lot of doors, though. After that my agents had a field day. All they had to say was that I was in "Carrie," and they wanted to see me. Then, when the movie came out and was a hit, it was even better.

JEWEL: Did that part get you into "Halloween"?

P.J.: John Carpenter wanted to see anybody who was in "Carrie." So I walked in and he had me read this scene, said "Great!" and that was it. It seems ridiculous now, considering how hard it is to get a part. But it was just the

130

ridiculous now, considering how hard it is to get a part. But it was just the circumstances at the time.

JEWEL: What was your part in "Halloween"?

P.J.: Jamie Lee Curtis and I and this other girl played teen-agers. And since I was going to bed with my boyfriend, I got killed. Pretty simple stuff.

JEWEL: Did "Rock 'n' Roll High School" come after those two films?

P.J.: After "Halloween," I did some TV stuff...I had to audition about four times for "Rock..." Alan Arkush really liked me but Roger Corman had his doubts. He just kept coming into the casting office and looking at me, but never saying anything. Finally he said, "She's okay if she makes her hair more blonde!" But I was really excited about doing that part because it was the last time I was going to get to play a teen-ager. I was twenty-eight at the time we did that movie...the only hard part was convincing myself that The Ramones were a band to die for! *(laughs)*

JEWEL: You got great reviews for that movie.

P.J.: It was funny, that movie was made for around $200,000 and Alan Arkush was under such pressure not to go over budget that on the last day of filming, they had to cart him away in an ambulance. Joe Dante stepped in and covered the last couple scenes...but I think he liked Dey Young better than me, because he kept featuring her in all the shots. I wanted to remind him that Riff Randall was the star of the film, but I was too nice to say anything.

JEWEL: You know, it seems like you've been in a lot of movies that started out like small B-movies but turned into hits.

P.J.: Yeah, I guess so. Actually, "Private Benjamin" was my first A-movie, since it had a real star. Originally, the director who hired me was fired and Howard Zeiff came in and said he wanted an all-new cast. But I just kept persisting until I heard they were doing final casting. So I showed up with a black wig — because Goldie didn't want someone else with blonde hair in a big

With Bill Murray in "Stripes" (1981)

role — and a very up-tight shirt because I wanted this part of the tattletale. Well, the secretary wouldn't let me in, but I insisted. So she calls in and says, "There's a bitch out here who wants to be seen. And she'd probably be perfect for the part 'cause she's such a bitch!" So they let me in and I told my story about how I'd been cheated out of a part. Howard just looked at me for a moment, then let me read. And he gave it to me right there. I jumped up, screamed and threw off my wig and he was like, "You mean that's not your real hair?" *(laughs)*

JEWEL: So when did you meet Dennis Quaid?

P.J.: Actually, I skipped a movie, "Our Winning Season." I did that after "Carrie." And that's where I met Dennis, when we were on location in Georgia. We got married right after that movie.

JEWEL: Was it love at first sight?

P.J.: Yeah, kind of. At first we thought it was just a location romance, but since neither of us had ever been on location before, it was hard to tell. I don't know, maybe we should have just left it at that...It was a sweet movie, though, and Dennis is great in it. It was a real showcase for him. Right after that, he got "Breaking Away."

JEWEL: How did you get "Stripes"?

P.J.: I had just finished doing a movie called "Soggy Bottom, U.S.A." — which was never released — and my agent called to say that the producers of "Stripes" were looking for the girl to play opposite Sean Young. Anyway, I flew over to Knoxville, Kentucky, and auditioned with Harold Ramis. I remember the driver who was taking me back to the airport said, "I've got a feeling I'm going to be picking you back up pretty soon." And I said, "I sure hope so."

JEWEL: So that was perfect, jumping from one film to the next.

P.J.: Yeah, it sounds so easy, but...usually there's so much time between projects where you just sit around wondering what you're going to do. I usually spent time on the set with Dennis, which was nice because I didn't really like long separations of more than two weeks. Also, I felt nervous because he was four years younger than me and there's always so many girls around.

JEWEL: When did the marriage start falling apart?

P.J.: Actually, while I was doing "Soggy Bottom," he was doing "The Night the Lights Went Out in Georgia." We were apart for three months and it was really hard. After I finished "Stripes," we took three months off and toured the Far East. But when we came back he did "The Right Stuff." That was our fifth year, when the problems really started. Dennis didn't want me hanging around the set anymore...

JEWEL: How was it working with Bill Murray in "Stripes"?

P.J.: It was hard. He's very funny, but he's very moody. Once the camera was rolling, he was great...that scene in the kitchen with both of us was completely improvised because Ivan Reitman said he needed a scene where we got together, something "cute." So Bill started pulling out kitchen utensils and that's how it started.

JEWEL: Did you have any nudity in any of your films?

P.J.: Well, in "Carrie," we were all supposed to be naked in the shower scene, but since that was my first film, I sort of managed to hold up my towel. I didn't know how my body would photograph. But then in "Halloween," John said he needed something sexy...and that was fine.

JEWEL: What about violence? Do you feel that portraying violence conveys a negative image to the public?

P.J.: Well, now that I have a family, I don't think I would choose to do a lot of films that I did when I was younger. Now that my son is six, I see what influences him...I've always been sent scripts that I've more or less thrown up over and have turned down.

JEWEL: You produced a film, didn't you?

P.J.: Yes, it's called "B.O.R.N.," which stands for Body Organ Replacement Network. It actually was inspired by a series of articles which insisted that there is a huge black market for body organs, and that a lot of the kids who have been kidnapped are being used for body parts to supply rich people in need of transplants. My neighbor, Ross Hagen, came to me with the idea, and I helped him produce it. We shot a promo for it and raised the money from there. And I felt like, "Maybe that's what I'm going to do from now on."

JEWEL: You're married again now, aren't you?

P.J.: Yes, to Skip Holmes. He's a test pilot who worked on "The Right Stuff" with Dennis. Skip didn't know Dennis was married because apparently Dennis was kind of having this thing with Pam Reed, who played his wife in the film. Anyway, Skip was the one who took Dennis up for training and said to him, "If I can make you sick, can I have your wife?" Of course Dennis said he wouldn't get sick, but as it turned out Dennis threw up in his helmet — which had this microphone attached to it — and when Skip started talking to the control tower, Dennis thought he was trying to talk to him so he put the helmet back on! *(laughs)* So he lands with this stuff dripping down his face...anyway, Skip got out and said, "I think I won the bet."

JEWEL: So did you start dating Skip after the divorce?

P.J.: Well, he called me up, but I wasn't ready to see another guy yet. But within two months, we were madly in love. And he wanted to have children, which Dennis and I weren't able to do. So we have two kids...and now I feel like I just want to pursue a normal life, because actresses get treated very strangely in Hollywood.

With Don Johnson in "Soggy Bottom, U.S.A." (1982)

133

"It started with 'Slumber Party Massacre,' where I got stabbed and had to run off and hide...there's a lot of adrenalin flowing and I really geared myself up for the scene by drinking a lot of coffee and hyperventilating."

Brinke Stevens

Across the country, almost every weekend, science fiction and comic book fans gather for conventions, mostly to meet favored celebrities from the world of s-f and horror movies, funnybooks, Star Trek and the like. But no one, not even Spock himself, attracts as long a line of autograph hunters as does Brinke Stevens, carrying on the fine tradition of the "Scream Queen." In the few years that Brinke has been before the cameras — much of that time spent getting chopped-up and/or showering — she has racked up an impressive résumé of low-budget films. With some of these movies, production values are so low that about all they have going for them is the appeal and personality of the stars...and it is in this capacity that Brinke has distinguished herself. Her roles have ranged from a spectacle-eyed nerd who boasts of owning the world's largest Lava Lamp in "Sorority Babes in the Slimeball Bowl-a-Rama" to a crazed old woman in "Grandmother's House." She has worked extensively as a print model and dancer, as well, and currently publishes a newsletter for the many members of the Brinke Stevens Fan Club.

JEWEL: I've always been curious. What nationality are you?

BRINKE: Three quarters German, one quarter Mongolian. But I grew up in a rural part of San Diego. It took an hour and a half to get to school. Our bus went through all the back communities, picking up one person here or there.

JEWEL: What did your parents do all the way out there?

BRINKE: My mother was an executive secretary for Travelodge, so we got to stay there for free whenever we traveled. My dad was a contractor who fixed up houses. We moved about once a year, but usually only a block away. I just hated packing all the time.

JEWEL: Were you popular in high school?

BRINKE: Not at all. I was really shy. If someone spoke to me, I blushed and looked away. Plus, I was really smart and into science fiction, two things which count against you. Everyone thought I was weird because when "Star Trek" was on I cut my bangs straight across like Mr. Spock had.

JEWEL: *(laughs)* You what?

BRINKE: I also trained my eyebrows to grow up like he had. I wanted to be a Vulcan. They had no emotions and they were really bright. I was the perfect

Vulcan...But it wasn't until high school that I started to come out of my shell a little bit...my teachers made me get up and speak in front of class. Eventually, I was elected senior Christmas Princess, which was my final coming out. It was a big deal, and I was really honored that my classmates finally liked me.

JEWEL: So you were ridiculed throughout most of high school?

BRINKE: Actually, no. They mostly just left me alone. I think they were afraid of me. In grade school, it was worse because the teachers liked me and put me on accelerated programs. I was using ninth grade math books in sixth grade and it drove the other kids crazy. They would take my books and dump them in the trash cans. Then I'd start crying and the teachers would have to console me. I was completely ostracized in grade school.

JEWEL: How was college for you?

BRINKE: Much better. I finally was in my element. There was a Star Trek club and everything! *(laughs)* I had a double major in Biology and Psychology. Then after four years at San Diego State, I enrolled in Scripps Institute of Oceanography where I applied for the Ph.D. program in Marine Biology. But because of various conflicts at school, I ended up leaving with only a Master's degree.

JEWEL: What kind of conflicts?

BRINKE: I told them right from the beginning that I wanted to work with dolphins, but they told me flat out that it wasn't a politically smart thing to work on...this was back in 1978, and there was about one thousand dolphins a day being killed in tuna nets. Now, San Diego was a big tuna fishing center...so obviously, nobody wanted to speak with dolphins but me. But at the same time I started going down to Sea World, where two baby dolphins had just been born. I was studying the dolphins to compile a dolphin research library. Well, somehow word got back to the people at Scripps and they called me onto the carpet and said I couldn't stay there. They told me it would've been safer if I'd stuck to guppies, and they made me leave.

JEWEL: What did that do to you?

BRINKE: I felt like my whole world had just ended. I cried and walked on the beach and went on unemployment...I felt like my whole life was over. I wanted to go to Hawaii and live the rest of my life as a research scientist with a big tank full of dolphins, but my whole future had been shattered with that dismissal from graduate school. Anyway, I became a beach bum for a while until I met this photographer who told me I was really pretty. He took some photos of me and pretty soon I got better and better. We even got a few jobs doing ski wear and things like that.

JEWEL: So you were off and running...

BRINKE: Well, the fellow I had been dating in San Diego, Dave Stevens, moved to L.A. and was working for Steven Spielberg as a storyboard artist on "Raiders of the Lost Ark." Dave said, "Why don't you leave San Diego, come on up to L.A. and marry me?" So I got married, but I still didn't have a job. And I couldn't find any biology jobs...then about six months later our marriage broke up and I suddenly found myself in Los Angeles in an empty apartment, without a job, without a husband. So for the second time in less than two years, my whole world was shattered. I didn't know what to do...and since I couldn't find a biology job, the only other experience I had was modeling. I started sending out photographs and bought an answering machine, which was really my only

piece of furniture. It was sink or swim.

JEWEL: Did you get into bathing suit modeling, or did you stray down that path so many of us did?

BRINKE: Yes, I did. I did a couple things for *Penthouse* and a couple of things for *Playboy*. I also did legitimate things too, though, like modeling eyeglasses for optometrists.

JEWEL: Were you a Playmate?

BRINKE: No. I did a girl-girl thing for *Penthouse*, and for *Playboy* I did "The Girls of Rock 'n Roll" and "Flashdancers," but I've never been a centerfold. They all said the same thing; that my breasts weren't big enough...but I wasn't about to change them.

JEWEL: The Girls of Rock 'n Roll? Were you in a band?

BRINKE: Well, I had met Linnea at a bunch of auditions and we became friends. At the time, she was in this band called The Skirts and her bass player had a broken wrist. So, when Linnea went to this audition for a movie about an all-girl band, she asked me to go along. I became the new member of The Skirts even though I didn't play the bass...but I did play the guitar as a kid, until my parents sold it one day. I used to have this fantasy where I'd sing along with The Monkees records, using my hairbrush as a microphone. So The Skirts was kind of like living out my fantasy. But it was short lived because both of us were getting more and more into acting.

JEWEL: What was your first feature film?

BRINKE: Well, I'd made an appointment with a modeling agent out in The Valley. I had my portfolio with me, but the guy had forgotten. Needless to say, I was extremely dejected. Well, I'm trudging down the corridor and I pass this open doorway and there's a guy sitting behind this desk with a bunch of movie posters on the wall. He sees me and says, "You, with the book! Come here!" Turns out this guy is Jacob Bressler. He looks over my book and says I have a nice look. Next thing, he puts me in a movie called "All the Marbles" as an extra. So I continued working with Jacob, who was getting me lots of featured extra work along with some body double stuff. I did a lot of shower scenes in the beginning.

JEWEL: What, they would show the actress's face and then pan down to show your body?

BRINKE: Yeah. I did that in "Psycho III." I got this call because Diana Scarwid wasn't available to do these pick-up shots where her character's getting undressed right before she gets into the bathtub to slit her wrists. I put a blonde wig on, but you don't see my face, just the back of my body.

JEWEL: So when did you get into Vampirella?

BRINKE: I was still in San Diego and I'd been going to these science fiction conventions. There was this one called the San Diego Comic Con where they had people masquerading as comic characters. Well, I liked Vampirella. She was an alien vampire...

JEWEL: Then this was a real character?

BRINKE: It was a character that Forrest Ackerman created for the Warren Publishing Company, and I did it in 1973 at this convention. Well, Forry was one of the judges and I thought he'd be very upset that I was doing his character, but instead he was quite honored...I got first place for it and became good friends with Forry.

JEWEL: When did you become Evila?

BRINKE: After Forry Ackerman quit *Famous Monsters* magazine, he started a new magazine called *Monsterland*. But when he left that one too, the editors needed an editorial mascot with a personality so they created Evila — a cross between Elvira and Vampirella. Since they needed someone to bring her to life, the art director, who knew me from the Comic Con, suggested that I do it. So I became Evila. For a year I was on three of their covers and went to all the conventions, handing out magazines.

JEWEL: What was your first speaking role in a film?

BRINKE: When Dan Golden was at Forry's house one day, he saw a photo of me and said that I was the kind of girl he wanted for this student film he was doing, which was called "Zyzak is King."

JEWEL: What was this movie about?

BRINKE: It was a short film about gaming on computers. You know, like Dungeons & Dragons...I played a student named Sara who gets involved in one of these kind of games and enters this alternate reality where she becomes this fur clad barbarian witch. Then one of the boys gaming becomes Zyzak, this invincible warrior. Anyway, the warrior and the witch team up to overcome this horrible monster.

JEWEL: Did that lead to something bigger?

BRINKE: I got a part in "Slumber Party Massacre," right on the heels of "Zyzak." It was a Roger Corman movie. I only worked a week on it, getting $40 a day, but it was a good part. I had lines and everything. After that, I did "Sole Survivor," which gave me my S.A.G. card. And that's when I started to like what I was doing. I thought, "I don't know if I can act or not, so I'll just do it until somebody stops me." Well, I kept doing it more and more and nobody stopped me. Eventually, I started studying my tapes to try and get better, but I never really had any formal training.

JEWEL: When did you make the transition into leading roles?

BRINKE: Not until '86, when I did "Slave Girls from Beyond Infinity," written, produced and directed by Ken Dixon. It was a real low budget film, about $130,000. I got the part of Sheila, who wasn't one of the slave girls. She was a rich girl whose yacht crashes on this planet, who's forced to survive. It was the first film in which I really got to do something substantial...but the next year, I met Dave Dakota through Linnea and got "Sorority Babes in the Slimeball Bowl-a-Rama" and "Nightmare Sisters."

JEWEL: You did those with Linnea and Michelle Bauer...

BRINKE: Right. The three of us had really come together. We went from doing shower scenes in "The Man Who Wasn't There" to leads in these other films. And that's what I like about low budget films. You get a chance to stretch your wings and do something that you wouldn't be allowed to do in a big budget movie.

JEWEL: What is "Warlords"? I've never heard of that one.

BRINKE: "Warlords" was a Fred Olen Rey film. I'd met Fred for "Star Slammer," which I didn't get. But he called me in for "Warlords" and handed me a script. I ended up playing David Carradine's kidnapped wife. I wasn't in the film that much, but they talked about me the whole time. *(laughs)*

JEWEL: I don't know if you realized it, but we were both in "Naked Force," in which I think you had the same kind of "hardly seen" character. How did you get involved in that one?

BRINKE: Gary Graver, who'd been a cameraman on several of Fred Olen Rey's films, told me about the movie and said there was a part in it for a B-movie actress. He said, "It's kind of like Linnea Quigley." *(laughs)* I said, "Gary! I can play myself, thank you!" So I played this B-movie actress named Candy Johnson and you're right...it was another pivotal character you never see until the end of the movie, because I'm one of the killers...my character and Deanna Lund are supposedly lesbian lovers who get together and plot the murder of her husband.

JEWEL: Did you have to do anything with Deanna?

BRINKE: It was this extremely mild scene where we were both in robes on this bed with an uzi between us, and she's fondling the gun talking about murder. It wasn't really a lesbian scene at all.

JEWEL: I know you've done a lot of films for Fred Olen Rey. What are some you haven't mentioned already?

BRINKE: "Mob Boss" was one...It was close to one million dollars and it had a bunch of names in it: Morgan Fairchild, William Hickey, Stuart Whitman...I was hired for the part of a female assassin named Sara, who, along with her partner Angelo, played by Jack O'Halloran from the "Superman" movies, very ineptly tries to kill William Hickey. But we are so incompetent, we can't kill him. It was a lot of fun. Also, I did "The Haunting Fear" with Fred, where I played this wife who gets buried alive by her husband and his lover, but instead of dying, I break out of the coffin and kill them both. I had the lead role in that film, but because Jan-Michael Vincent and Karen Black have bigger names, they

From "Grandmother's House" (1988)

went above the title. Then, when Delia Sheppard became more visible from the "Rocky" movie she did, they took her name and put it above the title, too. I was really upset about that...But overall, Fred has given me the chance to play different kinds of characters. Not just bimbo girls who get killed.

JEWEL: Tell me about "Chinatown Connection."

BRINKE: It was a Yankee Classic Picture. I'd met the director on a small *Penthouse* vignette I'd done called "Ghost Town" where this Penthouse pet and I are driving through this ghost town and she gets seduced by the ghost of a cowboy while I spend the whole movie walking around looking for her...Anyway, I met Jean-Paul Ouellette, who said after "Ghost Town" that he always wanted to work with me again. So on "Chinatown Connection," he called me in and I played the wife of this oriental cop called Bruce Li, kind of the successor to Bruce Lee. In the original script, I was pregnant and kidnapped and in the end, I lost the baby. But they thought that was too mean-spirited, so they revised it so that I'm just pregnant, walking around opening doors and saying "Hi" to people.

JEWEL: *(laughs)* That sounds like the ultimate subservient role.

BRINKE: It was fine...I never reached the point where I got that high-horse mentality to judge the scripts I was doing. Because in all of them...I mean, in "Slave Girls," for goodness sakes, I was held down naked by robots on a dissection table and raped by this madman. You can't afford the luxury of judging the parts you play.

JEWEL: But don't you ever feel a responsibility towards the younger kids who see these films?

BRINKE: Now I do. But at the time I didn't really feel noticeable. Since I'm developing more of a following now, though, I do care. I still don't know how much control I can have over a film, but I can say when I don't feel that the violence is appropriate. For instance, one of the last films I did was "The Haunting Fear," where I was supposed to stab this girl repeatedly with a knife. Well, the director agreed that rather than show the blade going in, he would just show my face and my hand with the knife. That made me happy.

JEWEL: Has your stance changed on nudity?

BRINKE: Now that I'm in my thirties, I don't want to do it. My body's not as good as it was, and there's only a few more years when I'll be able to do it anyway! *(laughs)* At least now, I'm not being hired specifically to do the nudity and if they tried to do that, I'd turn it down. I just have more respect for myself now. Not that I'm being holier than thou, because nudity's fine. I have no problem with it. I just resent when it's the primary reason I'm being hired. No more shower scenes just for the money! *(laughs)*

JEWEL: What's up next for you?

BRINKE: A film in June called "Lady Vengeance." It has no nudity in it at all. It's being shot in Orlando by a company called Cine Mondo. Stuart Whitman plays a CIA agent and Monique Gabrielle and I play his sisters. It's a real action adventure movie, where we get to shoot crossbows and uzis. So I've been going to the gym every day to build up the muscles in my arms and legs, along with getting a tan.

JEWEL: Do you ever get a strange feeling, watching yourself in these movies?

BRINKE: Oh, yeah. I'm my worst critic.

JEWEL: *(laughs)* No, I mean seeing yourself get murdered and raped and whatever else. Does that bother you?

BRINKE: I still get enthralled and emotionally connected when I watch myself. It started with "Slumber Party Massacre," where I got stabbed and had to run off and hide...there's a lot of adrenalin flowing and I really geared myself up for the scene by drinking a lot of coffee and hyperventilating. So for a while, every time I saw the scene, I'd dig my nails into my palms and relive it. Now it's not so bad, but I'm still emotionally connected to my scenes.

JEWEL: But it doesn't bother you to depict violence and sex on the screen?

BRINKE: I'm sure I'll suffer criticism. In fact, one woman came up to me and said, "So, how does it feel to do pornography?" I said, "Excuse me?" And she said, "Well, you take your clothes off and that's pornography!" So I told her, "Pardon me, but I think we have slightly different views of pornography." But there's always going to be people who criticize what you do. They just don't realize I didn't write and direct these movies. I just acted in them!

JEWEL: But you are getting into writing, aren't you?

BRINKE: I've been involved in writing for years. I was editor of my junior high and high school papers and always got A's on my term papers. So when the opportunity came to write a script with a collaborator, Ted Newsone, who was given the job but didn't have enough time to finish it himself, I took it. It was a script called "The Recruiter" and we did it for Marco Garibaldi. It's never been made because it's a little too similar to "Robocop," but I worked on it with Ted, who taught me a lot about the script format. Then he offered me the chance to do an earthquake safety film, which I did myself. After that, I wrote "Teenage Exorcist," which I sold to A.I.P. It's a great thing to do when you're not acting...I've got a lot of science-fiction ideas that could be tailored for me to play the leading role.

JEWEL: Do you have any other hobbies?

BRINKE: I like to work with my hands. I do stained glass...the first one I did was this skull with a snake coming out of its eye sockets. At first, my mother was so delighted that I was learning stained glass, but then she saw my first project and said, "Oh sweetie, that's, uh...very nice." So, for her benefit, the next one I did was roses. I also make beaded bags to supplement my income.

JEWEL: I would imagine you have a fan club?

BRINKE: I don't know how people find me, but I get about ten letters a month. Most of them just say, "I really like your work. Please send me a photo." It's amazing to me that there are people out there who get a lot of excitement from connecting with one of their favorites. I'd think they'd go for the big stars, but I guess we're so much more accessible.

JEWEL: Any weird fans?

BRINKE: No. I've been blessed with really intelligent fans...radiation physicists, chemists. Amazing people. I even have this one teacher back East that teaches senior level high school...he caught a kid reading a *Monsterland* magazine in his class, so he confiscated it. Well, that night he read it and became enraptured with me. So he found out my address and wrote me a letter just to say hello. Turns out he ran a local science fiction convention called Rovacon in Roanoake, Virginia. And he invited me to come...

JEWEL: Is there something that would like to do to change the world?

BRINKE: After that convention in Roanoake, I told the kids that I was an environmentalist and I started giving them a speech about how the planet was in grave shape...and how they could make sacrifices, protest, recycle and so on.

From "Slave Girls From Beyond Infinity" (1987)

And that's the platform I'm taking right now because when more and more public spokespersons start taking the same stand, that's what's going to turn the tide. It's such a crucial issue for future generations.

JEWEL: Speaking of which, do you see kids in your future?

BRINKE: I'd like to, but I haven't found the right man. In fact, I've even considered just having a child...and a bunch of men quickly volunteered for that job! *(laughs)* But I realize how hard it is to raise a child by yourself. And once you're into your thirties, I think it's easier to have a child, than to find the right man to settle down with. If if doesn't happen, though, I think I can live an equally satisfying life by myself.

"There were so many opportunities that were there, but agents and managers sometimes get too busy and ignore them."

Yvette Vickers

One evening, at a party somewhere in Hollywood, director Billy Wilder overheard a woman laughing. The laugh so interested him that he determined, then and there, to cast the woman it was coming from as a laughing party guest in his next film. And so Yvette Vickers made her screen debut in a party scene in "Sunset Boulevard" —not a bad beginning, by any means. Forty-some-odd years later, she is still acting and, though she has appeared in TV shows and films to fill a long list, she is still best known to some film fans for "Attack of the Fifty Foot Woman" and "Attack of the Giant Leeches." It perhaps says something about Hollywood and type-casting that, when I interviewed her, she barely spoke about her appearances in "Hud" with Paul Newman, in "What's the Matter With Helen?" opposite Debbie Reynolds and Shelly Winters, and other "A" pictures.

JEWEL: Is Yvette Vickers your real name?

YVETTE: No. When I was younger, I got a part in a musical and the producer said to me that my surname — Van Vedder — was very confusing. He wanted something easy. So he pulled a name out of a phone book in the V section and came up with Vickers.

JEWEL: Were you born in California?

YVETTE: Actually, I came out here when I was six months old and I have lived here ever since. But I was born in Kansas City, Missouri.

JEWEL: What did your parents do?

YVETTE: They are musicians. My mother is a concert pianist and my father is a jazz saxophone player. Eventually, he taught her to play popular music and they did club dates together...but that was later. When I was growing up, they were mostly at home.

JEWEL: Did you attend all local schools here?

YVETTE: Yes, then I even went to college at U.C.L.A..

JEWEL: Were you popular in high school?

YVETTE: On and off. I was a mixed bag, terribly gregarious. They even called me "Curvy" because of my figure. But I realize now that it was with affection — especially when one of the nuns at the Catholic school explained it to me. There were two nuns I became very close with. They were my mentors. I even considered being a nun at one time.

JEWEL: Didn't you feel too sheltered in that environment?

YVETTE: Well, my father was a musician and he brought home a lot of men at night. So during the day, I had this conservative side, but at night these guys might play music all night long, and they treated me as a grown up. I loved the Bohemian environment. In fact, they taught me all the standards, which I sometimes got up and sang at school when things got boring.

JEWEL: When did you get your first boyfriend?

YVETTE: I dated even in high school. I met a wonderful fellow through a girlfriend and we fell in love. I was fifteen and he was twenty-two. That relationship spoiled me rotten...we were actually engaged. But he wanted to go to college, and because I had skipped a few grades, I was almost ready to go. As soon as I got to U.C.L.A., though, the whole world opened up for me. I started running from one social event to another...

JEWEL: Is that when you got interested in acting?

YVETTE: Yes, although I had always been fooling around with entertainment.

JEWEL: You did a spread in *Playboy*, didn't you? And Russ Meyer shot it.

YVETTE: Yeah, that was in '59. So much happened that year. I did two movies, I did a play on Broadway and a bunch of other photo shoots. I was in continual motion.

JEWEL: Being a Playmate in '59 must have been a shock to most people. You must've been considered a sex goddess!

YVETTE: Well, we'd already seen years and years of that thing...but it affects every man you meet. They think they can just walk up to you and say "I want you," and it will all come true. Fortunately, I was married.

JEWEL: But not to the twenty-two-year-old sweetheart.

YVETTE: No. First I married a musician. He was a bass player named Don Krell, who now plays for the San Francisco Symphony. Don was the reason I broke my earlier engagement. It lasted for two years, but I was too young to be married then.

JEWEL: What was your first movie?

YVETTE: "Shortcut to Hell" with James Cagney, who personally wanted me for the part. And that's when I really became dedicated as an actress.

JEWEL: How did James Cagney know about you?

YVETTE: I was doing a play, "Bus Stop," and my agent was so enthusiastic about my performance that he went to A.C. Lyles and Cagney at Paramount and told them about me. Even though they had another girl under contract, he got me an audition. So I did a scene from "Girl in a Biaflimina," this scene where this naive girl is trying to be a hooker but changes her mind when she falls in love with this possible client. Well, I brought tears to my agent's eyes...the scene is very poignant. Finally, Mr. Cagney agreed to see me and we hit it off like old friends. He said, "If you want to do this movie, you've got it."

JEWEL: Were you ever hit on by producers or directors who wanted you for more than just a part?

YVETTE: I always believed that if you're good at your work, you should succeed. So when it happened, I just tried to stay composed. There were two times I was actually chased around the desk. But I escaped and made such a fuss that neither of those men could ever see me again. Needless to say, I didn't get either job.

JEWEL: Getting back to the *Playboy* spread: Do you feel that it helped your career or hurt it? And is it possible that the *Playboy* photos gave men the wrong impression of you?

YVETTE: You know, I really don't know what that did for my career. Directors already knew me as a serious actress, but I guess I worried that other people might not know about my stage work. It's hard to say what affect it had really, on anything.

JEWEL: Earlier, you mentioned that you did two movies around the time of the *Playboy* spread...

YVETTE: I think that was just about the time I did "Reform School Girls" with Roger Corman.

JEWEL: Didn't you have any apprehensions about doing low budget films?

YVETTE: I figured that I could learn a lot more by doing...I just wanted the exposure. I remember one funny thing from "Reform..." There was a scene where I had to pick up a snake, and I hate snakes. I'm better now, but...anyway, I'm one of those people who says she'll do anything. So, of course, I said the snake was no problem. But then I actually had to touch this slithering thing! *(laughs)* It turned out great, though, because I did the scene with a lot of gusto. You know, we all took the movie so seriously, it was like we were doing an Elia Kazan film, not a Corman picture.

JEWEL: You've got a lot of great titles on your résumé: "The Giant Leeches," "Attack of the Fifty-Foot Woman." Didn't you feel silly doing these pictures, considering that you were trying to establish yourself as a serious actress?

YVETTE: I was in such a positive frame of mind in that time period, everything I did, I felt good about. I can't think about anything bad to say about those

Yvette Vickers with Paul Newman in "Hud" (1962)

films. I just went into each project with the attitude of, "This is a major film." Directing your career is something I didn't learn until very late. When I did these movies, I was still young. I thought my agents were doing the right thing. I just let them get me jobs because I was a workaholic. I wanted to work all the time. It didn't occur to me that this wasn't the way you worked up and got into A-movies. I wasn't aware that you already have to be in that class, and I wasn't aware of the politics of this industry.

JEWEL: Do you regret not taking the reigns of your career earlier?

YVETTE: I feel like I wasn't very smart about everything. There were so many opportunities that were there, but agents and managers sometimes get too busy and ignore them.

JEWEL: Do you have any humorous recollections of filming "Attack of the Fifty-Foot Woman?"

YVETTE: There wasn't that much time. We shot that in eight days. I was pretty much "One Take Yvette." I think one of the charms of the films is the special effects. The big plaster-of-paris hand, the giant you could see through...but when I was there on the set, I just pretended this was all real. I don't question it.

JEWEL: Were you asked to do a lot of nudity over the years?

YVETTE: Not until the seventies. I did a couple of favors for a few friends. The parts were small bit parts, but I think there was a coldness in the industry towards me, because this man I knew was planting rumors in the press about me picking up sailors and what-not...anyway, I never did any real nudity.

JEWEL: Are there any causes to which you add your name?

YVETTE: I belong to Actors For Animals, P.E.T.A., Greenpeace and the Sierra

149

Club. I try to be active in all of them. But with all of the things I'm caught up in right now, it's hard. I just have to make the time. If you say you believe, you have to act.

JEWEL: What are you caught up in right now?

YVETTE: I'm trying to record four more songs to go with the songs I've already got done. My music is kind of a chantuese, torchy blues...but with a lift. I was greatly influenced by Charlie Parker and Billie Holiday because my parents exposed me to that music from a young age.

JEWEL: How do your parents feel about your career?

YVETTE: They're happy. They just wish it would've gone higher. But I know I've been considered for some major roles...and I know I'm good on the stage, so that's where I'm putting my energy now, into live shows.

JEWEL: Is there anything you'd like to change about yourself?

YVETTE: What I learned I'm sure I learned at the right time and for the right reason. This is part of my spirituality. I believe things happen for a reason. Therefore, I have a very positive outlook for my future.

Yvette Vickers with Rory Calhoun in "The Saga of Hemp Brown" (1958)

"My mother...she'd rather see me fail so I would have to come spend the rest of my life living with her."

Mary Woronov

One of the great "bad guys" in the history of B-movies was a bad girl: Mary Woronov in the role of the rock-music-hating principal Ms. Togar in "Rock 'n' Roll High School" (1979) Though Mary had already made her mark in films as an occasional member of artist Andy Warhol's "rep company," it was as Togar that she drew rave reviews (and offers to play similar characters on TV and in other films). Years later, she teamed with director-actor Paul Bartel (who had also played a key role in "Rock 'n' Roll High School") and they starred as the Blands in Bartel's cult classic, "Eating Raoul." Financed on a shoestring and deferred salaries, "Eating Raoul" proved again that a clever script and acting can triumph over a lack of budget. Her screen appearances also include "Angel of H.E.A.T.," "Heartbeeps," and "The One and Only."

JEWEL: You grew up in Brooklyn Heights? I was born in Flatbush.

MARY: Oh, wow...small world.

JEWEL: What did your parents do?

MARY: My mother didn't do anything. After I turned six, my mother married Dr. Woronov. He was a cancer specialist who mopped up after other doctor's screw-ups.

JEWEL: Sounds pleasant. Did you enjoy your childhood?

MARY: Yeah, I had a good time. I mean, Elvis Presley had just sung "Hound Dog"...and I grew up with all that great rock 'n roll. I went to a private girls' school, so I didn't date much. But then, I used to go to this church, where I eventually met some boys. Harry Chapin, he went to the same church. So did Bobby Lam. They were my childhood sweethearts.

JEWEL: Was it your idea to go to an all-girls' school?

MARY: Let's put it this way: I became aware of the fact that girls at the Catholic school fucked. I mean, they were getting pregnant all the time. But I went to this private Protestant girls' school and they were very strict...I knew I was missing out on something when the grocery boy would come to our house, and he'd look really, really good!

JEWEL: When did you start to develop your fantasies of an acting career?

MARY: I didn't, really. I just dreamed of getting married. I mean, that's what all the songs were about back then. Falling in love.

JEWEL: Did you have any kind of social life?

MARY: Not really. We had teas with our brother school and there was the occasional ballroom dancing, but that was about it. These guys didn't dance to rock 'n roll. They were mostly intellectuals.

JEWEL: You didn't rebel against any of this?

MARY: Not really. And if you don't rebel, you come out of the whole experience pretty smart. I went to Cornell.

JEWEL: What did you study?

MARY: To get into Cornell, I had to apply as a sculpture major. This was when there were almost no girls at Cornell. I figured there would be lots of girls who knew history and math, but sculpture seemed like a safe bet. The truth is, I never imagined myself sculpting for the rest of my life.

JEWEL: When did you make the transition into film?

MARY: During my years at Cornell, they would take us around to various artists' studios. Well, one of the places we went was to Andy Warhol's studio. So I started making movies with him.

JEWEL: What was it like working with Warhol?

MARY: It was fun. It was wild. These queens were wild. They liked me...They took a lot of drugs, but I was already accustomed to drugs because my stepfather was a doctor and I could get any drugs I liked.

JEWEL: So you'd experimented with drugs?

MARY: Of course.

JEWEL: What did your parents think of all this?

MARY: I don't know. I mean, I brought Lou Reed home for breakfast once. They just thought he was nice. My parents were kind of wacky.

JEWEL: It's hard to imagine this little girl from a strict Protestant upbringing cavorting with Warhol. What about your friends from school? Weren't they shocked by any of this?

MARY: The girls that I went to high school with, by the time I was at Cornell,

"Let It Ride" (1989)

they were married. I had a boyfriend at Cornell who didn't want me to get involved in the whole scene, but that was just because he wanted me to sit around and be his girlfriend.

JEWEL: So what came after Warhol?

MARY: My big dilemma really was "How am I going to support myself?" I found out I could make money doing plays. Not much, but enough to live on. Eventually I got on a soap called "Somerset" and I made a lot of money. That's when it dawned on me that I could really be an actress.

JEWEL: Did you enjoy your experience on the soap?

MARY: The work was great. But all the people involved with the show were very unhappy, really unpleasant to be around.

JEWEL: Did that change your impression of acting?

MARY: No, because I'd done a play at The Lincoln Center called "In the Boom-Boom Room," and all the actors where were really happy. I even won an acting award for that play. But the funny thing was, the producers initially cast me as a chorus girl. I wanted the main role, but they gave it to a big star who was truly crazy. Then the producers started getting really nervous and asked me to understudy her role. The night before the first show, they fired her because she was literally insane. So that's how I got this part...but even right up to the end, the producers were still trying to replace me. Right up to the fucking end!

JEWEL: But you showed them, winning that award.

MARY: I guess I did...but I gave this stupid acceptance speech and thanked Joseph Papp and everybody else. I should've just told them all to go fuck themselves. Then again, maybe I shouldn't have...because that's how life is.

JEWEL: So you moved out to California?

MARY: When I first moved out here I couldn't get any work. I got scared and got married. Eventually, work started coming fairly steadily. I mean, my career has never been great. I've always done really wacko stuff and the people who make the big money movies tend to stay away from me. But I finally realized I could make enough money without being married, so I got rid of my husband.

JEWEL: How long did it take you to acclimate yourself to L.A.?

MARY: Not long. I really love L.A.. After the marriage, I started doing [Roger] Corman movies, then a few regular movies.

JEWEL: You've played a lot of tough characters. I remember this really wicked villainess you played in "Rock 'n' Roll High School."

MARY: In the sequel, too. And then there was that prison warden I played on "Charlie's Angels."

JEWEL: Let's talk about "Eating Raoul"...

MARY: I don't even know why I did that movie — I wasn't even getting paid. But at that time [in my life], I would do just about anything. Fortunately, it turned out to be a really good movie.

JEWEL: Were there any films you regretted doing?

MARY: There was this one film that my husband was making. It was kind of a soft-core porn movie, but not really. Anyway, I was supposed to play a queer. I never really understood why he wanted to cast me as a queer. It really bugged me...but I did it for him anyway, because he's put me in his first movie — this was his second film.

JEWEL: What were the names of these films?

MARY: Oh, they never came out...The first one was called "Chemic." The second one, I thought it was porno, but I guess it wasn't. It was called "Sugar Cookies." I understand that it plays in motels in the South. I didn't enjoy making it, but you know, it was my husband, so I figured, "What the hell?"

JEWEL: Were you a natural in front of the camera?

MARY: The first time was with Warhol. He'd put you on a stool with the camera about three feet away, pointing at you. Then they'd all leave... and the camera kept on rolling for five minutes. After the first couple minutes of being bored, your personality would come out...at least that's what Warhol believed.

JEWEL: Didn't that shock you at all?

MARY: None of it was really shocking to me. Back then, they exposed you to real experimental stuff in college...I knew what was art and what was shit. But sometimes the shit was more interesting.

JEWEL: Did you ever aspire to be a movie star?

MARY: That's like wishing you had ten children. You can't imagine what's it's like until it happens...and then it's too late.

JEWEL: Wasn't there ever a part you really wanted in a studio film?

MARY: The last part I really wanted, there was no way I could've gotten it. Jessica Lange was booked ahead of time for that part for years. You just have to realize, this industry is big business. It's not about fantasies coming true...

JEWEL: How did you get involved with Paul Bartel, the director of "Eating Raoul"?

MARY: He was a friend of my first husband's.

JEWEL: After "Eating Raoul" came out and became an underground classic, did it change your life any?

MARY: Not really. I mean, I'd already done another film, "Death Race 2000," that was an underground classic. But neither of those films were seen by huge amounts of people. Nor did they make huge amounts of money.

JEWEL: Is there any part, say in classic literature, that you have always wanted to play?

MARY: A couple. But what I've done is written something for myself. I know the ideal part for me will never just come along, so I created it myself.

JEWEL: Describe the main character.

MARY: She's a mother, who's absolutely insane and tries to kill her children. I mean, she doesn't actually go through with it, but she'd like to.

JEWEL: *(laughs)* Don't you ever want to play more...uh, normal roles?

MARY: Don't get me wrong. I'd like to play anything.

JEWEL: Through your career have you maintained any kind of family support?

MARY: No. My mother knows what I do, but I think she'd rather see me fail so I would have to come spend the rest of my life living with her. But frankly, she can wait until Hell freezes over...

JEWEL: Do you ever get fan mail?

MARY: Yes, but I don't answer it. I don't believe in fans. Especially not since Rebecca [Schaeffer] got killed... but I wasn't answering my fan mail before that. I just don't think there's anything about me they need to know. Not that I don't love my audience. I do. And I would knock my ass off to entertain them, but my personal life is private.

JEWEL: Looking around the walls in your place, I notice you do a lot of painting...

MARY: Well, after going to Cornell as an art major, I decided I should do it.

That's what I knew. So that's what I did. And throughout my acting career, I always got that attitude like "Oh, that was the last film I'll ever do." And I was right, sometimes I wouldn't work for months and months. So I've always turned to art.

JEWEL: When did you start showing your pieces?

MARY: In New York, it was not necessary to show your stuff. People came over to your place and saw it. If they liked it, they bought it. Here in L.A., I only started showing it recently.

JEWEL: Is it a rewarding experience, showing your art?

MARY: At first, I thought it was great. It was like acting. I loved it. But now I hate it. I don't think I'll ever show my stuff again. It just seems like it doesn't really matter. It just gets depressing when you show stuff and nobody buys anything. It's like, "Fuck this!"

JEWEL: But you told me you've sold some of your pieces?

MARY: Oh, yeah. But I have a circle of people who just come over to my place and buy from me privately. Besides, I'm not too keen on the art world right now.

JEWEL: You mentioned you wrote a script. Do you like writing, or was that a purely functional exercise to create an acting vehicle for yourself?

MARY: I've always enjoyed writing. But my shrink convinced me I need to just focus on one: either acting or painting or writing, and make the other two hobbies. I don't know...I have had some stuff published in the L.A. Weekly but that was under a pseudonym.

JEWEL: Do you have any non-creative hobbies?

MARY: I like swimming. I want to swim in the Pepperdine pool. (thinks) I like cars. I like driving... I used to have the greatest Trans Am.

JEWEL: Me, too!

MARY: Why do you wear so much make-up, Jewel?

JEWEL: (taken aback) Uh, my skin is going through hell right now...

MARY: Well you shouldn't. It makes your skin wrinkle funny.

JEWEL: (laughs) Back on the subject of you...have you ever had a brush with greatness?

MARY: I was in one of these bathhouses in town. And there was this woman in there. A pretty woman with nice tits. Anyway, I think she noticed I was staring at her and she came over to where I was sitting. She said, "You're Mary Woronov, aren't you? I really like your work." What was I supposed to say? "Why, thank you. And I like *your* tits?" *(laughs)* Then she introduced herself as Deborah Harry. My jaw almost dropped open. I'm standing there wise-ass naked with Deborah Harry and I had nothing to say to her. I mean, I love her singing, but I was just too fucking stunned.

JEWEL: *(laughs)* Okay...Last question. Is there any cause you've aligned yourself with?

MARY: I'm not a really good person to ask that question of...because in my mind, there is no future. Just a winding down of business...

Photo by Alisha Tamburri

Many of the actresses interviewed in this book have fan clubs. For more information, send a stamped, self-addressed envelope to the appropriate addresses.

Monique Gabrielle Fan Club
4520 Van Nuys Blvd., #538
Sherman Oaks, CA 91403

Becky LeBeau Fan Club
505 S. Beverly Dr., Suite 973
Beverly Hills, CA 90212

Kitten Natividad Fan Club
P.O. Box 48938
Los Angeles, CA 90048

Linnea Quigley Fan Club
13659 Victory Blvd., Suite 467
Van Nuys, CA 91401

P.J. Soles Fan Club
P.O. Box 2351
Carefree, AZ 85377

Brinke Stevens Fan Club
8033 Sunset Blvd., Suite 557
Hollywood, CA 90046

Yvette Vickers Fan Club
P.O. Box 664
Pinon Hills, CA 92372

For comments on this book, write to:

Jewel Shepard
P.O. Box 480265
Los Angeles, CA 90048

(If you wish to write to any of the other ladies covered in this book, write in care of the above address and we will attempt to forward your letter. But no promises.)